THE SPIRIT OF CHRISTMAS®

BOOK SIXTEEN

EDITORIAL STAFF

Vice President and Editor-in-Chief: Sandra Graham Case
Executive Director of Publications: Cheryl Nodine Gunnells
Publications Director: Kristine Anderson Mertes
Design Director: Cyndi Hansen
Editorial Director: Susan Frantz Wiles
Photography Director: Lori Ringwood Dimond
Art Operations Director: Jeff Curtis

DESIGN
Lead Designer: Diana Sanders Cates
Designers: Cherece Athy, Polly Tullis Browning,
   Peggy Elliott Cunningham, Anne Pulliam Stocks,
   Linda Diehl Tiano, and Becky Werle
Craft Assistant: Lucy Combs Beaudry

FOODS
Foods Editors: Celia Fahr Harkey, R.D., and Jane Kenner Prather
Copy Editors: Judy Millard and Laura Siar Holyfield

OXMOOR HOUSE
Editor-in-Chief: Nancy Fitzpatrick Wyatt
Executive Editor: Susan Carlisle Payne
Foods Editor: Kelly Hooper Troiano
Copy Editor: Donna Baldone
Editorial Assistant: Diane Rose
Contributing Intern: Megan Graves
Senior Photographer: Jim Bathie
Photographer: Brit Huckabay
Senior Photography Stylist: Kay E. Clarke
Photography Stylist: Ashley J. Wyatt
Test Kitchen Director: Elizabeth Tyler Luckett
Test Kitchen Assistant Director: Julie Christopher
Test Kitchen Recipe Editor: Gayle Hays Sadler
Test Kitchen Staff: Gretchen Feldtman, R.D.;
   Jennifer A. Cofield; David C. Gallent; Ana Price Kelly;
   Kathleen Royal Phillips; and Jan A. Smith

TECHNICAL
Managing Editor: Leslie Schick Gorrell
Book Coordinator and Senior Technical Writer: Jean W. Lewis
Technical Writers: Kimberly J. Smith and Theresa Hicks Young
Associate Technical Writer: Stacey Robertson Marshall
Technical Associate: Jennifer Potts Hutchings

EDITORIAL
Managing Editor: Alan Caudle
Senior Editor: Linda L. Garner
Associate Editors: Steven M. Cooper and Kimberly L. Ross

ART
Art Director: Mark Hawkins
Senior Production Artist: Mark R. Potter
Production Artists: Ashley Carozza, Matt Davis, Clint Hanson,
   Faith Lloyd, Lora Puls, Rhonda Shelby, Dana Vaughn,
   and Elaine C. Wheat
Staff Photographer: Russell Ganser
Staff Photography Stylists: Janna Laughlin and
   Cassie Newsome
Publishing Systems Administrator: Becky Riddle
Publishing Systems Assistants: Myra S. Means and
   Chris Wertenberger

PROMOTIONS
Designer: Dale Rowett
Graphic Artist: Deborah Kelly

"... and it was always said of him, that he knew how to keep Christmas well, if any man alive possessed the knowledge. May that be truly said of us, and all of us!"

— From *A Christmas Carol* by Charles Dickens

BUSINESS STAFF

Publisher: Rick Barton
Vice President, Finance: Tom Siebenmorgen
Director of Corporate Planning and Development:
   Laticia Mull Cornett
Vice President, Retail Marketing: Bob Humphrey
Vice President, Sales: Ray Shelgosh
Vice President, National Accounts: Pam Stebbins

Director of Sales and Services: Margaret Reinold
Vice President, Operations: Jim Dittrich
Comptroller, Operations: Rob Thieme
Retail Customer Service Managers: Sharon Hall and
   Stan Raynor
Print Production Manager: Fred F. Pruss

Library of Congress Catalog Card Number 98-65188
Hardcover ISBN 1-57486-239-1
Softcover ISBN 1-57486-293-6

10 9 8 7 6 5 4 3 2 1

CONTENTS

CONTENTS

THE SHARING OF CHRISTMAS

Page 56

THE TASTES OF CHRISTMAS

Page 66

THE SIGHTS OF CHRISTMAS

Glittering ornaments, lush greenery, glowing candles, rich colors … the sights of Christmas are wondrous to behold! On the following pages, we'll show you how to create the perfect holiday setting by combining handmade trimmings with decorations you already have. You won't believe how easy it is to dress your home in stylish elegance, rustic simplicity, or icy grandeur!

Easy Elegance

Hosting an easy and elegant party for your closest friends is one of the nicest things you can do for yourself at Christmas. This is the heartfelt sentiment of Jeanne Spencer, an avid believer in the soul-nurturing power of longtime traditions and relationships. Join us as this congenial hostess demonstrates how to have a relaxing, memorable party.

Jeanne likes to delight guests, even before they reach the door, with warm outdoor lighting and imaginative holiday displays.

Decorating the dining room can be a leisurely activity when done early in the day, or even a day ahead. To complement Jeanne's English décor, we hung a lush garland above the doorway and dressed it with painted magnolia leaves, berries, and fancy ribbon. (Tip: Heavy-duty suction cup hooks are great for wall swags.) The table's beribboned centerpiece is simply a bowl of assorted greens embellished like the garland, with added swirls of sheer ribbon and glass ball ornaments attached with floral picks. More garland extends the greenery to each corner of the table, and Tussie-Mussies accent all the chairs.

With the centerpiece low to allow good conversation flow, each setting is marked with a Gold-Embossed Place Card and a Ribbon Napkin Ring trimmed with evergreen.

Instructions for Easy Elegance begin on page 118.

A prettily decorated table near the door makes a "favor-able" impression, especially when it's bearing fancy Party Favors to give each guest as they depart. We cut and folded elegant wrapping paper to make these ribbon-tied bags, then filled them with chocolates and other little treasures. For a festive look, we nestled the bags among greenery and berries on tiers created by stacking three glass cake stands.

At the door, an evergreen wreath trimmed with silver and gold magnolia leaves and ribbon sets the tone for this inviting party, while pepperberry wreaths add lively color to the windows. You can find ready-made pepperberry wreaths at hobby and floral shops, or craft your own: simply glue berry sprigs to miniature moss or grapevine wreaths.

As guests arrive, usher them inside to chat beside appealing tables laden with tasty appetizers and sparkling drinks.

PARTY TIP
Encourage guests to mingle throughout your home … arrange hors d'oeuvres and drinks in the living room, set the dining room for a sit-down dinner, and serve coffee and dessert in another cozy spot. And don't forget — little touches such as scented candles, festive towels and soaps, and evergreen swags over mirrors and frames add to the holiday atmosphere.

Along with your favorite appetizers, try new treats like savory Almond-Bacon-Cheese Crostini or spicy Mongolian Beef Skewers *(recipes on page 17)*.

You can easily create attractive candle rings to coordinate with your décor. In a glass bowl or vase, surround a hurricane globe candleholder with wet floral foam. (Tip: To add height, use floral clay to secure the candleholder atop an inverted votive holder.) Arranging longer pieces on the outside and shorter ones on the inside, insert sprigs of fresh Christmas greenery into the foam. Position several glass ornaments upside down by wiring their caps to floral picks, and loop ribbon through the arrangement.

Instructions for Easy Elegance begin on page 118.

Making Christmas ornaments for a community tree or to give loved ones is an annual tradition for these longtime friends, whose high school reunion group evolved into a garden club. Jeanne's family tree, sparkling with more than 2,000 keepsake trimmings, includes some of the ornaments she's made at the gatherings. "I have no problem putting very inexpensive ornaments next to more costly ones," she confesses. "What's important is that every one represents something very special to me." Among them are the crib mobiles and every childhood ornament made by Jeanne's son and daughter, pleated foil tree light collars from an estate sale, handmade dough shapes, and a shiny gold department store gift tag — her favorite of all, because of its message, "I love you baby, Daddy." Many ornaments reflect Jeanne's interest in her Greek heritage, and others are simply dated wooden discs cut from the trunks of every live Christmas tree the family ever displayed. How does Jeanne turn her diverse collection into such an impressive sight? She puts the lights on first and three types of garlands; then she starts hanging the smallest items at the top and graduates to the largest at the bottom. And she always crowns the tree with a golden angel identical to ones on the trees of her mother and brother. If only these tree trimmings could talk, just imagine the heartfelt stories they'd tell!

After dinner, move the party to the kitchen to combine coffee and dessert with a bit of Christmas creativity. These simple Beaded Ornaments are so quick to craft that the merry-making doesn't have to miss a beat.

Instructions for Easy Elegance begin on page 118.

Candlelight lends a warm glow to an easy-to-do Buffet Arrangement that enhances the dining experience. By preparing some things ahead, like the Rich Seafood Casserole and the batter for the Spoon Rolls, you can enjoy more time with guests. "The recipe for a successful party is to invite people you really love to be with, so make all the planning easy on yourself," Jeanne says.

Instructions for Easy Elegance begin on page 118.

MONGOLIAN BEEF SKEWERS

This simple appetizer is especially easy to serve. Soy sauce, fresh ginger, and sesame oil impart an Asian accent.

2½ pounds flank steak
½ cup hoisin sauce
2 tablespoons peanut oil
2 tablespoons sesame oil
2 tablespoons dry sherry
2 tablespoons soy sauce
½ teaspoon sugar
½ teaspoon pepper
½ teaspoon grated fresh ginger
1 clove garlic, crushed

Slice steak diagonally across grain into ⅛-inch-thick strips. Place in a large heavy-duty, resealable plastic bag. Set aside.

Combine hoisin sauce and remaining 8 ingredients; stir well. Pour marinade over steak; seal bag securely. Marinate in refrigerator 8 hours, turning occasionally.

Thread steak onto 32 (6-inch) wooden skewers. Discard marinade. Broil 3 inches from heat (with electric oven door partially opened) 2 to 3 minutes on each side or to desired degree of doneness.
Yield: 32 appetizers
Note: Unlike metal skewers, wooden skewers can burn under the broiler. Make sure to soak wooden skewers in water at least 10 minutes before threading food on them to prevent any flare-ups.

ALMOND-BACON-CHEESE CROSTINI

1 French baguette
4 slices bacon, cooked and crumbled
1 cup (4 ounces) shredded Monterey Jack cheese
⅓ cup mayonnaise
¼ cup sliced almonds, toasted
1 tablespoon chopped green onions
¼ teaspoon salt
    Garnish: toasted sliced almonds (optional)

Slice baguette into 36 (¼-inch-thick) slices. Arrange slices on an ungreased baking sheet; bake at 400 degrees for 6 minutes or until golden brown.

Combine bacon and next 5 ingredients in a small bowl; stir well. Spread cheese mixture on slices; bake at 400 degrees for 5 minutes or until cheese melts. Garnish, if desired. Serve immediately.
Yield: 3 dozen slices

WINTER SALAD WITH CRANBERRY VINAIGRETTE

CRANBERRY VINAIGRETTE

½ cup fresh cranberries
⅔ cup tangerine juice
⅓ cup tarragon vinegar
2 tablespoons Dijon mustard
2 shallots, minced
½ teaspoon salt
½ teaspoon pepper
½ cup walnut oil or light olive oil

SALAD

¾ cup pecan halves
⅔ cup honey
¼ cup butter or margarine, melted
½ cup sugar
8 kumquats
4 cups torn red leaf lettuce
4 cups finely shredded radicchio
3 seedless tangerines, peeled and sectioned
   Cranberry Vinaigrette
1 cup fresh mint leaves, shredded
   Garnish: fresh mint sprigs

For vinaigrette, bring cranberries and tangerine juice to a boil in a medium saucepan over medium heat; boil 5 minutes. Drain, reserving juice. Set cranberries aside. Return juice to pan, and simmer 5 minutes.

Process juice, vinegar, and next 4 ingredients in a blender until blended. With blender running, add oil in a slow, steady stream. Stir in cranberries.

For salad, stir together first 3 ingredients; spread evenly in a shallow roasting pan. Bake at 325 degrees for 12 to 15 minutes, stirring often. Remove pecans with a slotted spoon; toss pecans with sugar. Cool.

Cut kumquats in half lengthwise. Toss together lettuce, kumquats, radicchio, and next 3 ingredients. Sprinkle with pecans, and garnish, if desired.
Yield: 8 servings

RICH SEAFOOD CASSEROLE

Fresh shrimp and scallops come to the buffet baked in a Swiss cheese and wine sauce. Spoon over rice to serve.

- 1½ pounds unpeeled large, fresh shrimp
- 1½ cups dry white wine
- ¼ cup chopped onion
- ¼ cup fresh parsley sprigs or celery leaves
- 1 tablespoon butter or margarine
- 1 teaspoon salt
- 1 pound bay scallops
- 3 tablespoons butter or margarine
- 3 tablespoons all-purpose flour
- 1 cup half-and-half
- ½ cup (2 ounces) shredded Swiss cheese
- 1 tablespoon lemon juice
- ¾ teaspoon lemon pepper
- 1 (7-ounce) can sliced mushrooms, drained
- 1 cup soft whole wheat bread crumbs
- ¼ cup grated Parmesan cheese
- ¼ cup sliced almonds
- 2 tablespoons butter or margarine, melted
  Hot cooked rice

Peel and devein shrimp. Set aside.

Combine wine and next 4 ingredients in a Dutch oven; bring to a boil. Add shrimp and scallops; cook 3 to 5 minutes or until shrimp turn pink. Drain shrimp mixture, reserving ⅔ cup broth.

Melt 3 tablespoons butter in Dutch oven over low heat. Add flour, stirring until smooth. Cook, stirring constantly, 1 minute. Gradually add half-and-half. Cook over medium heat, stirring constantly, until mixture is thickened and bubbly. Add Swiss cheese, stirring until cheese melts. Gradually stir in reserved broth, lemon juice, and lemon pepper. Stir in shrimp mixture and mushrooms.

Spoon mixture into a lightly greased 11 x 7 x 1½-inch baking dish. (If desired, cover and chill overnight. Let stand at room temperature 30 minutes before baking.)

Cover and bake at 350 degrees for 40 minutes. Combine bread crumbs and next 3 ingredients; sprinkle over casserole. Bake, uncovered, 10 minutes. Let stand 10 minutes before serving. Serve over rice.
Yield: 8 servings

SPOON ROLLS

- 1 package dry yeast
- 2 tablespoons warm water (100 to 110 degrees)
- ½ cup vegetable oil
- ¼ cup sugar
- 1 large egg, beaten
- 4 cups self-rising flour
- 2 cups warm milk or water (100 to 110 degrees)

In a small bowl, dissolve yeast in 2 tablespoons warm water; let stand 5 minutes. In a large bowl, stir together yeast mixture, oil, sugar, egg, flour, and milk until a soft dough forms.

Cover tightly, and refrigerate at least 4 hours or up to 4 days. Preheat oven to 350 degrees. Stir batter. Spoon into greased muffin pans, filling three-fourths full. Bake 25 minutes or until golden brown. Remove from pans, and serve immediately.
Yield: about 20 rolls

RASPBERRY CORDIAL

- 2 (10-ounce) packages frozen raspberries in light syrup, thawed
- 1¾ cups sugar
- ¾ cup water
- 3½ cups brandy

Combine raspberries, sugar, and water in a medium saucepan; cook mixture over medium-high heat until sugar dissolves. Bring mixture to a boil; reduce heat, and simmer 5 minutes. Remove mixture from heat; let cool. Pour raspberry mixture into a 1-gallon jar. Add brandy and stir well. Cover mixture tightly and store in a dark place at room temperature at least 2 weeks. Shake jar gently once daily.

Pour mixture through a wire-mesh strainer lined with 2 layers of cheesecloth into a glass container with a lid, discarding raspberries. Cover tightly. Store at room temperature.

Use in beverages, trifles, or sauces.
Yield: 4¾ cups cordial

COCONUT-CHOCOLATE-ALMOND CHEESECAKE

- 1½ cups chocolate wafer cookie crumbs (28 to 30 cookies)
- 3 tablespoons sugar
- ¼ cup butter or margarine, melted
- 4 (8-ounce) packages cream cheese, softened
- 3 large eggs
- 1 cup sugar
- 1 (14-ounce) package flaked coconut
- 1 (11.5-ounce) package milk chocolate morsels
- ½ cup slivered almonds, toasted
- 1 teaspoon vanilla extract
- ½ cup (3 ounces) semisweet chocolate morsels
  Garnish: toasted chopped almonds and shaved chocolate (optional)

To form crust, stir together first 3 ingredients; press mixture into bottom of a 10-inch springform pan. Bake at 350 degrees for 8 minutes. Cool.

Beat cream cheese, eggs, and sugar at medium speed with an electric mixer until fluffy. Stir in coconut and next 3 ingredients. Pour filling into prepared crust. Bake at 350 degrees for 1 hour. Cool on a wire rack.

Place semisweet morsels in a resealable plastic bag; seal. Submerge bag in warm water until morsels melt. Snip a tiny hole in 1 corner of bag; drizzle chocolate over cheesecake. Cover and chill 8 hours.

Store in refrigerator up to 5 days. Garnish, if desired.

Yield: 10 to 12 servings
Note: We used Nabisco chocolate wafers.

Experiment with candleholders in varying heights to achieve a formal balance for the mantel. A loosely arranged garland of juniper and a scattering of gilded magnolia leaves provide natural contrast to gleaming stars, golden spheres, and candles of gold and cream.

A bed of dusky galax leaves and vibrant holly form a handsome setting for a glowing pillar. Use floral tape to affix faux galax leaves around the edge of a pedestaled cake stand, then wire holly sprigs together and place on top. If your stand has a depression in the center, add water to keep the holly fresh.

Candle Light, Burning Bright

A s twilight descends on a wintry eve, the flickering glow of candlelight casts its magic over your home. You can easily create a candlescape to remember, whether it's set amidst your finest crystal and gilded accents or simply displayed with fresh greenery.

Golden stars lend holiday elegance to plain glass votives. Use gold pearl liquid leading to draw the designs.

For a quick fix, tie a trio of candles with ribbon and showcase on a delicate Beaded Doily draped on a cake stand.

(Right, from top) Dressing a 3-wick candle in holiday style couldn't be easier … tie with sheer wire-edged ribbon, glue on a silk holly sprig, and display on a beveled mirror tile! Inexpensive beads add festive sparkle to pretty Spiral Beaded Tapers, and you can customize the Hurricane Candleholder by simply choosing a candle and bead garlands in colors to match your décor.

Burgundy and cream candles in an assortment of shapes and sizes add eclectic charm to a table. Try using pieces of glassware from your collection … dessert cups, candy dishes, bowls, and of course, candlesticks … to display your candles. Accessorize with scraps of gimp, ribbon, tassels, greenery, and beads — just grab a glue gun and use your imagination!

Instructions for Candle Light, Burning Bright are on page 121.

Lakeside Cabin Christmas

Nestled around a secluded lake, a little community of cabins offers a beautiful setting to enjoy the peace and love of the Christmas season. As you breathe in the crisp, clean air and listen to the rustle of winter birds in the branches overhead, it's easy to forget the holiday hustle and bustle. Join us now on a tour of several of these cabins, and whether you're planning your own winter getaway or decorating a city home in rustic style, you'll come away with an array of decorating inspirations for nature lovers.

Simple bundles of greenery and pinecones, attached using floral wire, add cheer to the fence, and Candle-Lit Lanterns provide a welcoming glow.

Instructions for Lakeside Cabin Christmas begin on page 122.

Natural Noel

As you step onto the deck of this traditional cabin, you're treated to a live potted tree trimmed in natural style and topped with a primitive star. We purchased a weathered metal star and sponged it with thinned orange paint to heighten its rusted look, but you could also cut your own shape from flashing and "age" it by lightly spraying with dark brown paint and then partially sanding with steel wool before sponging with orange. *(Right)* Colorful apples, pomegranates, and pears are nestled amid sprigs of evergreen and holly in an old metal colander.

Bright berries and evergreen sprigs add a festive touch to this Gourd Birdhouse.

Winding its way through the tree is a Natural Garland threaded on coils of rusted craft wire. We found the metal pockets and miniature sap buckets at a craft shop, sponged them with thinned paint in shades of greenish-brown, pine, and sage, and tucked in dried apple slices. The ready-made metal mittens and stars were given the same treatment as the treetop star. To create the little gourd birdhouses, paint black circles for "doors," then insert twig perches and wire hangers into small holes you've drilled. Tiny cedar birds, faux bird nests, and fresh holly round out the decorations.

Candles nestled in flowerpots gently illuminate the porch steps. To give terra-cotta pots an aged look, sponge-paint them like the mini sap buckets and finish with sealer (for fire safety, don't apply the sealer to the inside of the pots). Fill pots about halfway with sand, then place votives in the center.

Instructions for Lakeside Cabin Christmas begin on page 122.

Lakeside Getaway

Luxurious evergreen swags provide a fragrant welcome at the front door of this lakeside getaway. We used a variety of greenery, including white pine, balsam fir, cedar, juniper, and holly, for our outdoor decorations. You can purchase greens from a nursery, or take a walk through the woods and cut your own (be sure to ask permission from the property owner first). For the door swag, arrange several boughs with stems overlapping in the center, then secure with florist wire. Dress up smaller bundles with red multi-loop bows.

On a sunny day, a rocking chair on the dock issues an invitation to snuggle up with a blanket and enjoy the view of the lake. To make the chairback bouquet, secure boughs of evergreen and holly with floral wire and add a cheery bow. Additional bouquets for each of your dining chairs can help you continue this country-fresh holiday style indoors.

To re-create our window swags *(opposite)*, select a "draping" greenery (we used white pine) and cut boughs in varying lengths. Enhance the natural flare by gathering with the stems of the shorter ones up and the longer ones down; wire together. If you want a fuller, textured look, top with several boughs of evergreen (we added balsam fir). Tie strands of natural raffia to pinecones and hang from the front of the swag; finish with a big bow.

Even the overhead lighting fixture can become a festive focal point. Secure sprigs of greenery with floral wire and suspend metal twig ornaments from red ribbon.

Black felt bears look right at home on the chamois cuffs of the Fleece Stockings. The stocking pieces are blanket-stitched together for a no-fuss finish.

Glowing candles and lush evergreens usher visitors into a cozy holiday haven as they step through the door. A chairful of simply wrapped gifts heightens the hospitable mood.

Even if you don't have an entry hall, you can create a welcoming scene with baskets overflowing with evergreen cuttings and a bowlful of vibrant apples.

Instructions for Lakeside Cabin Christmas begin on page 122.

Twinkling lights follow a shining trail around the tree, accompanied by a garland of natural netting and strands of wooden beads. Easy-to-make Chamois Ornaments tied with leather lacing are complemented by red glass balls and ribbon-tied metal twig ornaments. The roughly carved wooden tramp-art discs and treetop star add to the rugged appeal.

Bear silhouettes amble about the Fleece Tree Skirt, which can be crafted with very little sewing! Primitive blanket stitch accents the cut fringe of the skirt.

A blazing fire in the hearth, stockings hung by the chimney, candles alight … the great room invites visitors to settle in for the festivities. The mantel overflows with an abundance of greenery and berries, with red tapers flanking an evergreen wreath decorated with naturals.

Instructions for Lakeside Cabin Christmas begin on page 122.

Cottage Charm

Cottage décor brings uplifting style to this airy enclosed porch. Decorative Birdhouses, candles, and a little nest add interest to a side table. We used scraps of chenille and rag rugs to stitch the comfy pillows. The Holly Leaf Pillow is accented with embroidery, Rag Pillows have plush fringe, and the flap of the Envelope Pillow was cut from an old quilt. A garland of greenery and berries runs all along the ceiling, coordinating with the tabletop tree and the hanging Ceiling Tile Pocket filled with evergreen and holly.

Instructions for Lakeside Cabin Christmas begin on page 122.

Starry Evening

A thick blanket of pine needles carpets the ground in a small clearing near the boathouse. Tiny white lights twinkle amid a "forest" of small potted evergreens, while candles flicker inside galvanized buckets of sand or lanterns … a magical site for an intimate dinner. Silvery stars, cut from flashing and loosely wrapped with lengths of 16-gauge galvanized wire, gleam among the trees. The table is draped with classic white linens and a colorful vintage quilt. White pillar candles in wire holders, small boughs of greenery, and berry sprigs form a

pleasing centerpiece. At each place setting, a miniature galvanized pail — a perfect party favor — holds a napkin, greenery, and an after-dinner chocolate.

Winter Majesty

A crackling fire and lush evergreens provide the perfect contrast for the cool elegance of this winter-white collection. The exquisite beaded ornaments and accessories, crafted in tones of silver and frost, will bring an air of shimmering sophistication to your holiday décor.

Snowy satin ribbon, frosted glass orbs, and crystal beads adorn these majestic accents and tree. To make a fitting foundation for the tree, we gave an inexpensive plaster urn a marbled finish like that of the pedestal shown on page 41.

Create a stately display for the foyer … paint a plaster stand to make an impressive Faux Marble Pedestal *(left)* and top it with a large silver bowl overflowing with boughs of evergreen and holly. Then nestle an assortment of snow-white ornaments atop the rich greenery and wind loops of sheer wire-edged ribbon through the arrangement *(below)*. We selected several Frosted Balls with Beaded Collars, Frosted Snowflake Ball Ornaments, Beaded Swirl Ball Ornaments, and a flurry of beaded snowflakes.

Instructions for Winter Majesty begin on page 130.

(Left) Beautiful packages, elaborately tied with shimmering wire-edged ribbon and floral picks of frosted evergreen, are artfully arranged on a swath of white voile beneath the tree.

Keep a familiar tradition in elegant style with our Tucked Cuff and Tucked and Beaded Stockings, lovingly crafted using tucked silk fabric and enriched with sparkling beads. They'll bring joy for generations to come!

(Right) For a striking tabletop arrangement, place candles of varying heights in a bed of greenery. Scatter with crystal snowflakes and frosted ornaments, and twine a glittering garland throughout.

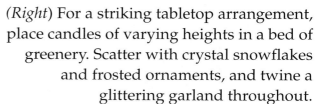

It's said that no two snowflakes are exactly alike … and these handcrafted Crystal Snowflake Ornaments can be just as unique! Follow our patterns to create the four distinctive designs, then add your own special touches. The beautiful Beaded Snowflake Ball Ornaments are surprisingly easy to make.

Delicate Beaded Gift Bags are
sewn from sheer fabric and
accented with bead stars.

Instructions for Winter Majesty begin on page 130.

Dress the mantel in winter finery — blanket a lush evergreen garland and wreath with twists of organdy ribbon, garlands of silver wire and glass beads, and frosty petals of crystal wisteria. Then use floral wire to attach pearly glass balls, twinkling snowflakes, and lengths of silvery tinsel.

Glistening Swirled Glass Icicles, made by gluing silver seed beads to clear ornaments, are a graceful option for your décor.

(Opposite) Matching in miniature: "Planted" in a silvery ice bucket, this charming tabletop decoration echoes the beauty of the splendid full-size evergreen. We added greenery picks to the tiny tree for fullness, then trimmed it with ribbon, garlands, crystal wisteria, and a blizzard of snowflakes.

Instructions for Winter Majesty begin on page 130.

Adorn your mantel in holiday style! To re-create our garland, use floral wire to secure fresh greenery and holly sprigs to a length of heavy jute. Hot glue pinecones to garland as desired. Soak spiraled grapevine garland in water until it's pliable, then loosely wind it around the greenery. To complete the setting, display your favorite dinner plates with decorative chargers and fill an array of bowls with fruit and candles.

Naturally Christmas

What could be more natural than Christmas in the country? But even if you're city-bound this holiday, you can create a farm-fresh atmosphere with fragrant evergreens, crisp, colorful fruit, and rustic accents.

A wooden bowl overflowing
with boughs of evergreen, sprigs
of holly, pinecones, and luscious
apples is sure to inspire Christmas
spirit. Line the bowl with heavy-
duty plastic wrap and fill with
water-soaked floral foam; arrange
elements as desired. Water often
and mist lightly to freshen.

An ironware pitcher holds a casual
spray of greenery and fruit. Cut a
piece of foam to fill your container;
tape in place, if needed, and add
water. Arrange tall evergreen sprigs
at the back and sides, then place
fruit on picks for the center and fill
in with cedar and holly until foam
is covered. Hot glue assorted nuts
to picks and tuck in to accent.

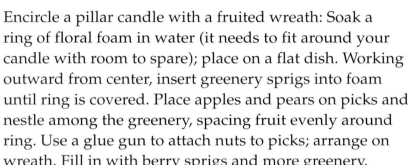

Make sure the larder is well stocked with staples, including canning jars filled with nuts for munching. Tie with raffia and accent with greenery.

Encircle a pillar candle with a fruited wreath: Soak a ring of floral foam in water (it needs to fit around your candle with room to spare); place on a flat dish. Working outward from center, insert greenery sprigs into foam until ring is covered. Place apples and pears on picks and nestle among the greenery, spacing fruit evenly around ring. Use a glue gun to attach nuts to picks; arrange on wreath. Fill in with berry sprigs and more greenery.

To make a simple swag for the wall, use grapevine and boughs of cedar, bind with wire at the center, and attach pinecones.

Flea Market Fancies

Create a cheery setting using flea market treasures with nostalgic appeal! Scope out yard sales during the year to collect metal gelatin molds, vintage holiday tablecloths, and memorabilia — then follow our easy suggestions to incorporate them into your seasonal décor.

Flea markets offer an abundance of ephemera, or paper art, including beautiful holiday postcards. To showcase these treasures, you can craft colorful paper "frames" — simply cut two pieces of card stock in graduated sizes (both larger than your card), layer with the card on top, and glue together. We used scallop-edged scissors to trim the inner border and added "stitches" with a fine-point marker. For hanging, glue a ribbon loop with long streamers to the back. Accent the front with a bow.

A well-dressed hearth imparts a cozy atmosphere to the room, and our colorful Fireplace Ensemble lets you make use of old holiday table linens. When your fireplace isn't lit, shield it with a festive screen decorated with felt and motifs cut from an old print tablecloth; save a border piece to create a no-sew mantel scarf. To complete the mantelscape, tuck sprigs of evergreen and mistletoe between bright red candles and nostalgic figurines. Anchor the setting with a pair of pretty vases filled with crimson silk roses and greenery (you'll find lots of inexpensive vases at flea markets).

Instructions for Flea Market Fancies begin on page 138.

For a tree that's bursting with cheer, start with a garland of faux mistletoe and then wind strips of lace trim among the branches. The button-drop "icicles" are a snap — loosely thread buttons onto narrow silver cord, creating a hanging loop at the top and reinforcing the bottom button with double stitching; then glue another button to the back of each one to stabilize. Scatter red silk roses here and there for added color (secure with floral wire, if needed). The gaily lit Starry Tree Topper provides a charming *pièce de résistance.*

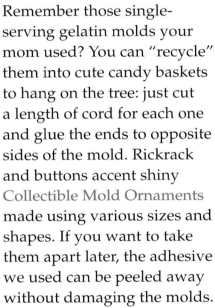

Remember those single-serving gelatin molds your mom used? You can "recycle" them into cute candy baskets to hang on the tree: just cut a length of cord for each one and glue the ends to opposite sides of the mold. Rickrack and buttons accent shiny Collectible Mold Ornaments made using various sizes and shapes. If you want to take them apart later, the adhesive we used can be peeled away without damaging the molds.

Treasured family photos enjoy a place of honor in a Window Frame made from a battered junk-shop find.

The Vintage Tablecloth Tree Skirt is a great way to recycle damaged linens … you can hide stains or holes in the pleats and gathers.

Don't forget the best use for your collectible molds — making yummy treats! Prepare your favorite fruitcake recipe and bake in individual tins, then decorate with icing and share with friends.

Household linens are so versatile! Our trio of Christmas pillows, all crafted from pieces of old tablecloths, include a ribbon-tied Bolster Pillow, a fringed Square Pillow, and a Round Pillow embellished with a crocheted potholder. You could also use oversize napkins, table runners, or doilies … just use your imagination!

Instructions for Flea Market Fancies begin on page 138.

THE
SHARING
OF
CHRISTMAS

*Sharing is the heart
of Christmas, and what
better way to show
you care than with a
handmade present?
A cozy hat and scarf
will keep a little girl
warm and toasty, while
a special host or hostess
will love a set of beaded
charms to help guests
keep track of their
wine glasses. Or for
a special family,
try a personalized,
hand-painted decorative
plate! We have a great
selection of gifts to warm
the hearts of family
and friends.*

Time to Rejoice!

Remind someone special that it's always "time to rejoice" with this DÉCOUPAGED CLOCK! Cut a pretty motif from a greeting card or wrapping paper for the face, then glue on a handful of star-shaped buttons for the finishing touch.

Découpaged Clock instructions are on page 141.

Light Up the Season

You don't have to be an artist to create one-of-a-kind gifts like this "JOY" CANDLEHOLDER — just paint an unfinished wooden candlestick with bands of color, then draw a simple star and freehand designs. Top it with a fragrant pillar candle and you're ready to spread Christmas cheer!

"Joy" Candleholder instructions are on page 141.

The gardener on your list will sing praises for this ANGEL FLOWERPOT TREE! Crowned with a joyful little angel, the terra-cotta "tree" is encircled with garlands of grapevine and berries and sprinkled with gilded papier-mâché stars … a charming display for the porch or sunroom.

Angel Flowerpot Tree instructions are on page 142.

Memory Bouquet

Share Christmas memories with a
CARD AND PHOTO DISPLAY filled with
fresh greenery and shiny ornaments, along
with wire photo holders bent into tiny tree
shapes and spirals. You can easily dress
up an inexpensive plastic planter to hold
your arrangement — just dry brush it
with paint and glue on a pretty ribbon.

Card and Photo Display instructions are on page 142.

Linen Keeper

Help a hostess keep her best
table linens neat and crisp with an
old-fashioned NAPKIN PRESS.
Pre-quilted fabric in a festive print and
ribbon ties make it especially nice.

Napkin Press instructions are on page 142.

Charming Accents

Here's to Christmas cheer! Designed to dress up party glasses, these brightly colored spangles are sure to inspire eloquent toasts. Experiment with different sizes and shapes of beads, making each BEADED CHARM unique help guests keep track of their drinks. An assortment of these accents makes a thoughtful gift for someone who enjoys entertaining.

Beaded Charms instructions are on page 143.

In the Name of Fun

Featuring a snowy friend, this HAND-PAINTED CERAMIC PLATE will quickly become a holiday treasure! The staff at your local ceramic shop will be happy to help you select and prepare a greenware plate that you can personalize for a special family.

Hand-Painted Ceramic Plate instructions are on page 143.

Cozy Snow Blossoms

Any little girl (or even a big girl!) would love this cozy HAT AND SCARF adorned with fleecy "snow blossoms." You could use our posy-making technique to dress up a seasonal sweater, too!

Hat and Scarf instructions are on page 143.

Taking a walk on the wild side couldn't be easier! For this FLEECE-TRIMMED JACKET, start with an unadorned jacket and stitch on a cozy fleece collar, cuffs, and pocket trim (we chose a nubby black jacket and zebra-print fleece). It's a great accessory for a fashion-conscious friend.

Fleece-Trimmed Jacket instructions are on page 144.

Holiday Hostess Set

This year, why not surprise your hostess with a festive bath set? Select a wintry fragrance to scent RUBBER STAMP SOAPS, and transform everyday linens into HOLIDAY HAND TOWELS edged with rickrack and buttons. You can use the same rubber stamp motif to decorate both the soaps and the GIFT TAG!

Rubber Stamp Soaps & Gift Tags and Holiday Hand Towels instructions are on page 144.

North Woods Wrap

Who wouldn't love to snuggle by the fire wrapped in this APPLIQUÉD THROW? It's easy to make by embellishing a ready-made fleece afghan with "North Woods" shapes and edging them with simple embroidery stitches.

Appliquéd Throw instructions are on page 144.

THE TASTES OF CHRISTMAS

*Festive family feasts
and elegant open houses,
impromptu dinners
and casual get-togethers …
everyone knows that the
best part of Christmas
merry-making is the food!
Check out our selection
of recipes for fresh, new
dishes to delight your
guests, along with tried-
and-true favorites. And
since nothing says "Happy
Holidays" like a home-
baked treat, we've included
several delicious gift ideas,
too. Get ready, get set,
and get cooking!*

Home for Christmas

Welcome everyone home for the holidays with a truly memorable feast featuring elegant beef tenderloin, mouth-watering sides, and a delightfully fruity bread pudding drizzled with warm whiskey sauce. Our convenient timetable makes it easy for you to prepare a perfect meal … and still have time to visit with your family!

MUSHROOM-ROSEMARY BEEF TENDERLOIN

- ¾ cup Marsala wine
- 1 shallot, minced
- ¼ cup olive oil
- 2 tablespoons red wine vinegar
- ½ teaspoon salt
- ½ teaspoon pepper
- 1 beef tenderloin (5 to 6 pounds), trimmed
- 1 pound fresh mushrooms, sliced
- 1 bunch green onions, sliced
- 1 tablespoon chopped fresh rosemary
- 2 cloves garlic, chopped
- 3 tablespoons butter or margarine, melted
- ½ cup Marsala wine
- 1½ cups soft whole wheat bread crumbs
- ½ teaspoon salt
- 2 teaspoons freshly ground pepper
- 8 slices bacon
  Garnish: fresh rosemary sprigs

In a small bowl, combine first 6 ingredients; stir well. Place tenderloin in a large shallow dish; pour wine mixture over tenderloin. Cover and marinate in refrigerator overnight, turning occasionally.

In a large skillet, sauté mushrooms, green onions, rosemary, and garlic in butter over medium heat until tender. Add ½ cup wine and simmer until liquid evaporates. Remove from heat. Add bread crumbs and toss gently. Set aside.

Remove tenderloin from marinade; discard marinade. Slice tenderloin lengthwise to, but not through, the center, leaving 1 long side connected.

Preheat oven to 425 degrees. Spread stuffing mixture into opening of tenderloin, spreading to within ½ inch from edge. Roll up, jellyroll fashion, starting at long end. Arrange bacon slices in a crisscross pattern over tenderloin. Tie securely with heavy string at 2-inch intervals. Sprinkle with salt and pepper. Place tenderloin, seam side down, on a rack in a roasting pan. Insert meat thermometer into thickest portion of tenderloin.

Bake, uncovered, 45 to 50 minutes or until meat thermometer registers 145 degrees (medium-rare). Cut strings and remove from tenderloin. Loosely cover tenderloin with aluminum foil and let stand 10 minutes before slicing. Garnish with fresh rosemary sprigs, if desired.
Yield: about 10 to 12 servings

For a beautiful presentation, Mushroom-Rosemary Beef Tenderloin is spiraled with herbed stuffing and baked to a perfect medium-rare. Oyster lovers won't be able to get enough of the Wild Rice and Oysters casserole, and frozen bread dough gives you a head start when making savory Parsley-Garlic Rolls (recipes on pages 70 and 72).

WILD RICE AND OYSTERS

- 1 quart chicken broth
- 2 packages (6 ounces each) wild rice
- ½ cup butter or margarine, melted and divided
- 1 small onion, chopped
- 2 ribs celery, chopped
- 1 pound fresh mushrooms, sliced
- 2 quarts oysters, drained
- ½ cup all-purpose flour
- 1 cup chicken broth
- 1 cup whipping cream
- 1 to 1½ tablespoons curry powder
- ½ teaspoon salt
- ¼ teaspoon pepper
- ¼ teaspoon hot sauce
- ½ cup chopped fresh parsley

In a large saucepan, bring chicken broth to a boil. Add rice; cover tightly and simmer 50 to 55 minutes. Drain rice after cooking if all chicken broth is not absorbed; discard broth. Toss rice with 2 tablespoons melted butter.

Sauté onion and celery in 2 tablespoons melted butter until tender. Add mushrooms and sauté 5 minutes. Remove vegetables from skillet. Set aside. Add oysters to skillet and simmer 2 to 3 minutes until edges of oysters begin to curl; drain well. Set aside.

Pour remaining 4 tablespoons butter into a large, heavy saucepan or Dutch oven. Add flour, stirring until smooth. Cook over low heat 1 minute, stirring constantly. Gradually add 1 cup chicken broth and whipping cream; cook over medium heat, stirring constantly, until mixture is thickened and bubbly. Stir in curry powder and remaining 4 ingredients. Add wild rice, vegetables, and oysters, stirring well; spoon into a lightly greased 9 x 13-inch baking dish. Preheat oven to 350 degrees. Bake 30 minutes or until bubbly.
Yield: about 10 to 12 servings

For the best flavor, be sure to use fresh beans when making Butter-Pecan Green Beans.

BUTTER-PECAN GREEN BEANS

- 2½ pounds small fresh green beans
- 1½ teaspoons salt, divided
- ⅓ cup butter or margarine
- ½ cup chopped pecans
- ¼ teaspoon freshly ground pepper

In a Dutch oven, cook green beans with 1 teaspoon salt in boiling water to cover 8 minutes or until crisp-tender; drain. Plunge into ice water to stop the cooking process; drain again.

In a large skillet, melt butter; add pecans and sauté until butter is lightly browned. Add green beans; sprinkle with remaining ½ teaspoon salt and pepper.
Yield: about 10 servings

LAYERED SWEET POTATO AND CRANBERRY CASSEROLE

If you're looking for a new side dish for the holidays, we recommend this cranberry and sweet potato casserole.

- 4 **large sweet potatoes (about 3½ pounds)**
- ½ **cup firmly packed brown sugar**
- 1 **tablespoon butter or margarine**
- 1 **cup fresh cranberries**
- ½ **cup orange juice**
- ½ **cup chopped walnuts**
- 2 **tablespoons butter or margarine, melted**
- 1 **tablespoon brown sugar**
- ½ **teaspoon ground cinnamon**

Cook potatoes in boiling water to cover 40 to 45 minutes or until tender. Drain and let cool slightly. Peel and cut into ¼-inch slices. Preheat oven to 350 degrees. Arrange half of sweet potato slices in a greased 9 x 13-inch baking dish. Sprinkle with ¼ cup brown sugar; dot with 1½ teaspoons butter. Top with ½ cup cranberries. Repeat layers. Pour orange juice over top. Cover and bake 45 minutes.

Combine walnuts, 2 tablespoons melted butter, 1 tablespoon brown sugar, and cinnamon; stir well. Sprinkle walnut mixture over potato mixture. Bake, uncovered, an additional 10 minutes.

Yield: about 8 to 10 servings

Orange juice enhances the sweet, tangy goodness of our Layered Sweet Potato and Cranberry Casserole.

BREAD PUDDING WITH WHISKEY SAUCE

We think you'll agree this is one of the best bread puddings around — so good that it received our highest rating.

BREAD PUDDING

- 1 loaf (1 pound) dry French bread
- 4 cups milk
- 4 large eggs, beaten
- 2 cups sugar
- 2 tablespoons vanilla extract
- 1 cup raisins
- 2 apples, peeled, cored, and cubed
- 1 can (8 ounces) crushed pineapple, drained
- ¼ cup butter, melted

WHISKEY SAUCE

- ½ cup butter
- 1 cup sugar
- ⅓ cup bourbon, divided
- 1 large egg, beaten

For bread pudding, preheat oven to 350 degrees. Tear bread into small pieces; place in a large bowl. Add milk to bowl; let mixture stand 10 minutes. Stir mixture well with a wooden spoon. Add eggs, sugar, and vanilla; stir well. Stir in raisins, apples, and pineapple. Pour butter in a 9 x 13-inch baking pan; tilt pan to coat evenly. Spoon pudding mixture into pan. Bake, uncovered, 55 to 60 minutes. Remove from oven and cool slightly.

For sauce, cook butter in a large heavy saucepan just until melted; add sugar and cook over low heat until smooth. Add half of bourbon and simmer 3 minutes; stirring well. Increase heat to medium low and gradually whisk in egg; whisk well. Remove from heat and let stand 2 minutes. Stir in remaining bourbon. Serve bread pudding warm with whiskey sauce.

Yield: about 16 servings and 1⅓ cups sauce
Note: To dry out fresh bread, preheat the oven to 200 degrees; tear bread into small pieces and bake 1 hour, turning once.

PARSLEY-GARLIC ROLLS

Put your own spin on convenient frozen bread dough with these little swirls. Pungent garlic and snippets of fresh parsley dress them in a savory fashion.

- 2 tablespoons chopped fresh parsley
- 3 tablespoons butter, melted and divided
- 2 cloves garlic, pressed
- ½ package (32 ounces) frozen bread dough, thawed

Combine parsley, 2 tablespoons butter, and garlic. Set aside.

Roll bread dough into a 12-inch square; spread parsley mixture over dough, leaving a ½-inch border on top and bottom edges. Roll dough tightly, jellyroll fashion, from bottom edge. Press top edge of dough into roll to seal edge. Cut roll of dough into 1-inch slices. Place slices, cut side down, in greased muffin pans. Brush dough with remaining 1 tablespoon butter.

Cover and let rise in a warm place (80 to 85 degrees), 1 hour or until doubled in size. Preheat oven to 400 degrees. Bake 9 to 11 minutes or until golden. Remove from pans and serve immediately.
Yield: about 1 dozen rolls

Be sure to save room for dessert — you'll want to enjoy every bite of this Bread Pudding with Whiskey Sauce!

Menu Prep Plan

Refer to this planning guide to make smart use of your time when preparing this holiday meal for 10 people.

1. Day Before: Prepare marinade for tenderloin; cover and marinate overnight. Prepare wild rice for casserole and chill overnight.
2. Day of Serving: If needed, dry out fresh French bread for pudding by tearing it into pieces and baking at 200 degrees for 1 hour.
3. Prepare Parsley-Garlic Rolls. Cover and let them rise for 1 hour or until doubled in size.
4. Cook potatoes for Layered Sweet Potato and Cranberry Casserole.
5. Meanwhile, remove rice from refrigerator and let come to room temperature. Sauté vegetables for tenderloin and prepare stuffing mixture. Toss rice with 2 tablespoons melted butter.
6. Peel and slice potatoes; prepare casserole.
7. Preheat oven to 350 degrees. Continue with preparation for Wild Rice and Oysters.
8. Preheat second oven, if available, to 425 degrees. Spread stuffing mixture into tenderloin; place bacon slices in a crisscross pattern over tenderloin and secure with heavy string. Place in a roasting pan.
9. Prepare Bread Pudding with Whiskey Sauce.
10. Bake tenderloin 45 to 50 minutes.
11. Meanwhile, blanch Butter-Pecan Green Beans. Set aside.
12. Fifteen minutes into baking time of tenderloin, put Layered Sweet Potato and Cranberry Casserole into 350-degree oven. After 15 minutes, add Wild Rice and Oysters.
13. Finish preparation of green beans; keep warm.
14. When tenderloin is done, reduce heat to 400 degrees and add rolls. Bake 9 to 11 minutes. Let tenderloin sit 10 minutes before slicing.
15. Remove other casseroles from oven.
16. Put Bread Pudding in oven as you sit down to dinner.
17. Reheat sauce just before serving dessert.

A Festive Gathering

An open house provides the perfect opportunity to share a bit of cheer with friends and neighbors! Dress your home in holiday finery — inside and out — and provide plenty of seating that encourages partygoers to mingle throughout the house. Plan a casual buffet of hors d'oeuvres and desserts, including our incredibly rich Hot Crab Dip and a delectable chocolate Yule log. For cocktails, you can serve mugs of Four-Fruit Wassail as guests arrive, or refer to our handy guide to set up an open bar. Let the festivities begin!

SWEET POTATO ANGEL BISCUITS

- 3   packages quick-acting dry yeast
- ¾   cup warm water (100 to 110 degrees)
- 7½ cups all-purpose flour
- 1   tablespoon baking powder
- 1   tablespoon salt
- 1½ cups sugar
- 1½ cups vegetable shortening
- 3   cups canned mashed sweet potatoes

In a 2-cup liquid measuring cup, dissolve yeast in ¾ cup warm water; let stand 5 minutes.

In a large bowl, stir together flour, baking powder, salt, and sugar; cut in shortening with a pastry blender until mixture is crumbly. Stir in yeast mixture and sweet potatoes just until blended.

Turn dough onto a lightly floured surface and knead about 5 minutes or until dough becomes smooth and elastic. Place dough in a well-greased bowl, turning once to coat top of dough. Cover and chill 8 hours, if desired.

Roll out dough to ½-inch thickness; use a 2-inch round cutter to cut out biscuits. Freeze up to 1 month, if desired. Thaw biscuits; place on ungreased baking sheets. Cover and let rise in a warm place (80 to 85 degrees) 20 minutes or until doubled in size.

Preheat oven to 400 degrees. Bake 10 to 12 minutes or until lightly browned.

Yield: about 7½ dozen biscuits

BAKED HAM WITH BOURBON GLAZE

- 1   cup honey
- ½   cup molasses
- ½   cup bourbon OR ½ cup orange juice
- ¼   cup orange juice
- 2   tablespoons Dijon mustard
- 1   smoked ham half (6 to 8 pounds)
     Garnish: fresh rosemary sprigs

Microwave honey and molasses in a 1-quart microwave-safe glass dish on high power (100%) 1 minute. Whisk to blend. Whisk in bourbon, ¼ cup orange juice, and mustard.

Preheat oven to 350 degrees. Remove skin and fat from ham; place ham in a lightly greased 9 x 13-inch pan. Make ¼-inch-deep cuts in ham in a diamond pattern. Pour glaze over ham. Insert meat thermometer, making sure it does not touch fat or bone.

Bake ham, uncovered, on lower oven rack 2 to 2½ hours or until meat thermometer registers 140 degrees, basting every 15 minutes with glaze.

Remove from pan, reserving drippings if you'd like to serve them alongside ham. Cover ham and drippings and chill until ready to serve, if desired. Reheat both just before serving. Garnish platter with fresh rosemary sprigs.

Yield: about 12 to 14 servings

Tuck slices of Baked Ham with Bourbon Glaze inside fluffy Sweet Potato Angel Biscuits for hearty finger sandwiches. If you cook the ham the day before the party, you can simply slice it and either heat it or serve it chilled. The biscuits can be prepared well ahead of time and frozen, then thawed and baked.

TOMATOES ROCKEFELLER

1 quart cherry tomatoes
  Salt
¼ cup butter or margarine
½ cup diced onion
1 clove garlic, minced
1 package (10 ounces) frozen chopped spinach,
  thawed and well drained
½ cup freshly prepared bread crumbs
½ to 1 teaspoon salt
1 teaspoon chopped fresh thyme
½ cup freshly grated Parmesan cheese
2 large eggs, lightly beaten

Cut off tops of tomatoes; scoop out and discard pulp, leaving shells intact. Sprinkle shells lightly with salt; place upside down on paper towels to drain.

Preheat oven to 350 degrees. Melt butter in a large skillet; add onion and garlic and sauté until tender. Stir in spinach, bread crumbs, salt, thyme, cheese, and eggs; cook, stirring constantly, until eggs are set. Spoon mixture into tomato shells and place in a 7 x 11-inch baking dish.

Bake 12 to 15 minutes or just until lightly browned.
Yield: about 30 appetizers

A savory filling of spinach and Parmesan cheese makes Tomatoes Rockefeller simply irresistible! To prevent the stuffing from becoming soggy, squeeze the spinach between paper towels to absorb as much moisture as possible before combining with the other ingredients.

A round of Brie in a Braided Bread Wreath makes an impressive showing on your sideboard … and it's much easier to prepare than you'd think! When selecting your cheese, look for one that's plump and pliant to the touch, with pale brown edges on the rind.

BRIE IN BRAIDED BREAD WREATH

BRAIDED BREAD WREATH

½ **package (32 ounces) frozen bread dough, thawed**

BRIE

⅓ **cup sliced almonds**
⅓ **cup sesame seeds**
1 **Brie round (35.2 ounces)**
3 **tablespoons apricot or pineapple preserves**
½ **cup sweetened dried cranberries**
½ **cup diced candied pineapple**
2 **French baguettes, sliced**

For braided bread wreath, place 2 large baking sheets on oven rack, overlapping edges so that width of baking sheets is at least 15 inches; grease.

Divide dough into thirds; roll each portion into a 36-inch rope and braid. Grease outside of a 9-inch round cake pan and place in center of prepared baking sheets. Wrap braid around cake pan, pinching ends to seal.

Cover and let rise in a warm place (80 to 85 degrees) 1 hour or until doubled in size.

Preheat oven to 375 degrees. Place rack with bread in oven. Bake 18 to 20 minutes or until golden brown. Remove from oven; cool on a wire rack.

For Brie, preheat oven to 350 degrees. In a shallow pan, bake almonds and sesame seeds separately, stirring occasionally, 5 to 10 minutes or until toasted. (Do not burn.)

Trim rind from top of Brie; brush preserves over top. Arrange almonds, sesame seeds, cranberries, and pineapple over preserves in a spoke fashion. Place Brie in center of braided bread wreath; serve with toasted French baguette slices.

Yield: about 20 appetizer servings

HOT CRAB DIP

- 3 tablespoons butter or margarine, divided
- 2 shallots, minced
- 1½ tablespoons all-purpose flour
- ¾ cup milk
- ½ teaspoon salt
- ½ teaspoon ground white pepper
- 2 teaspoons freshly squeezed lemon juice
  Dash of Worcestershire sauce
- 1 pound fresh lump crabmeat, drained
- ½ cup whipping cream
- 1½ teaspoons dry sherry
- 1½ teaspoons cognac
  Assorted crackers or Melba toast to serve

In a heavy saucepan, melt 2 tablespoons butter over medium-high heat; add shallots and sauté until tender. Remove from saucepan and set aside.

Melt remaining 1 tablespoon butter in saucepan over low heat and whisk in flour until smooth. Cook 1 minute, whisking constantly, until thickened and bubbly.

Whisk in shallots, milk, salt, white pepper, lemon juice, Worcestershire sauce, crabmeat, whipping cream, sherry, and cognac; cook mixture over low heat until thoroughly heated. Serve dip warm with assorted crackers or Melba toast.

Yield: about 2½ cups dip

WALNUT COOKIES

- 1 cup butter, softened
- 1 package (14 ounces) granulated brown sugar
- 2 large eggs
- 1 teaspoon vanilla extract
- ½ teaspoon black walnut flavoring
- 3 cups all-purpose flour
- 1 teaspoon baking soda
- 1 teaspoon salt
- 2 cups chopped walnuts

In a mixing bowl, beat butter at medium speed of an electric mixer until creamy; gradually add brown sugar, beating well. Add eggs and flavorings, beating until blended.

Combine flour, baking soda, and salt; add to butter mixture, mixing well. Stir in walnuts.

Divide dough into 10 portions; shape each portion into a 10-inch roll on waxed paper. Cover and freeze 8 hours.

Preheat oven to 350 degrees. Cut each roll, while frozen, into ¼-inch-thick slices and place on lightly greased baking sheets. Bake 6 to 8 minutes or until lightly browned. Transfer to wire racks to cool completely.

Yield: about 33 dozen cookies

Note: Cookie rolls can be frozen up to 1 month.

FOUR-FRUIT WASSAIL

- 1 gallon apple juice
- 2 cups orange juice
- 2 cups pineapple juice
- ⅔ cup lemon juice
- 4 cinnamon sticks (4 inches each)
- 1 cup bourbon or brandy
  Garnish: cinnamon sticks

In a large Dutch oven, combine apple juice, orange juice, pineapple juice, lemon juice, and 4 cinnamon sticks. Bring mixture to a boil; reduce heat and simmer 30 minutes. Stir in bourbon.

Remove 4 cinnamon sticks from hot juice mixture. Garnish servings of wassail with fresh cinnamon sticks.

Yield: about 5 quarts wassail

Bar Essentials

Wines

White wines can be on the dry side, or they can be slightly sweet; avoid very sweet wines. Sauvignon Blanc, Reisling, Chablis, and Chenin Blanc are good possibilities. To help in planning, you can estimate that there are four (6-ounce) servings in each 750-milliliter bottle of wine.

Cocktails

A well-stocked bar is usually composed of the following: vodka, scotch, rum, gin, and bourbon, plus mixers, including sparkling water, club soda, tonic water, ginger ale, soft drinks, orange juice, and tomato juice. Each 750-milliliter bottle of liquor is equivalent to 17 drinks when 1½ ounces are used per drink. One 10-ounce bottle of mixer per person is usually sufficient. To save time, prepare ahead any beverages that can be made in quantity and chill until ready to serve. You may decide to offer one special cocktail during the evening, such as Four-Fruit Wassail. Some guests may prefer a refreshing beverage without liquor.

Beer

Many people prefer beer over wine or liquor. Offer a variety, including light beer, imported beer, and dark beer. Keep frosted mugs on hand.

Ice

Plan on purchasing about ¾ to 1 pound of crushed ice per guest.

Spiced with cinnamon and served hot, Four-Fruit Wassail is sure to be a hit! It's also delicious prepared without the alcohol. Be sure to bake several batches of yummy Walnut Cookies — they'll be gone before you know it!

HOLIDAY CHOCOLATE LOG

A traditional French Christmas cake, the Yule log or bûche de Noël, can be frosted with chocolate frosting and a fork pulled through the frosting to create the appearance of tree bark.

- 6 large eggs, separated
- ¾ cup granulated sugar, divided
- ⅓ cup cocoa
- 1½ teaspoons vanilla extract
- ⅛ teaspoon salt
- 2 to 3 tablespoons confectioners sugar
- 1½ cups whipping cream
- ⅓ cup sifted confectioners sugar
- ¼ cup cocoa
- 2 teaspoons instant coffee granules
- 1 teaspoon vanilla extract
  Sifted confectioners sugar

Preheat oven to 375 degrees. Grease a 10½ x 15½-inch jellyroll pan. Line pan with waxed paper; grease waxed paper. Set aside.

In a large mixing bowl, combine egg yolks and ½ cup granulated sugar; beat at high speed of an electric mixer 3 minutes or until thick and pale. Add ⅓ cup cocoa, 1½ teaspoons vanilla, and salt; beat at low speed until smooth. Set aside.

Beat egg whites at high speed until foamy. Gradually add remaining ¼ cup granulated sugar, 1 tablespoon at a time, beating until stiff peaks form and sugar dissolves (2 to 4 minutes). Gently fold beaten whites into egg yolk mixture. Spread batter evenly in prepared pan. Bake 15 minutes.

Sift 2 to 3 tablespoons confectioners sugar in a 10 x 15-inch rectangle on a cloth towel. When cake is done, immediately loosen from sides of pan and turn out onto sugared towel. Peel off waxed paper. Starting at narrow end, roll up cake and towel together; let cool completely on a wire rack, seam side down.

In a medium bowl, combine whipping cream, ⅓ cup confectioners sugar, ¼ cup cocoa, coffee granules, and 1 teaspoon vanilla; beat at high speed until stiff peaks form. Cover and chill 1 hour.

Unroll cake; spread with whipped cream mixture. Carefully reroll cake without towel. Cover and chill at least 1 hour. Place cake roll, seam side down, on a serving plate; sprinkle with additional confectioners sugar.

Yield: about 10 servings

For a grand finale to the evening, serve Holiday Chocolate Log with plenty of freshly brewed coffee. This traditional French dessert is best if you make it a day early and chill it until ready to present.

CRANBERRY AMBROSIA-CREAM CHEESE SPREAD

- 2 packages (8 ounces each) cream cheese, softened
- ¼ cup confectioners sugar
- 1 package (6 ounces) sweetened dried cranberries, divided
- 1 can (15½ ounces) crushed pineapple, drained
- 1 can (11 ounces) mandarin oranges, drained
- 1 can (3½ ounces) shredded coconut, divided
- 1 cup chopped pecans, toasted
- 8 pecan halves, toasted
  Gingersnaps to serve

Stir together cream cheese and sugar until blended. Reserving ¼ cup cranberries, add remaining dried cranberries.

Pat pineapple and oranges dry between layers of paper towels. Set oranges aside.

Reserving ¼ cup coconut, stir remaining coconut and pineapple into cream cheese mixture. Stir in chopped pecans. Spoon mixture into a serving bowl.

Sprinkle reserved dried cranberries around edges of bowl. Arrange orange sections around inside edge of cranberries. Sprinkle reserved coconut in center and top with toasted pecan halves. Serve with gingersnaps.

Yield: about 24 appetizer servings

Perfect Coffee

Make sure your coffeepot and coffee grinder are kept clean — any residue can give your brew a "stale" taste. Choose a high-quality coffee, whether you prefer whole beans or ground, and store in an airtight container in the refrigerator until ready to use. When preparing coffee, always use fresh, cold water, never hot or boiling! Make sure you use the proper proportion of coffee to water: The standard ratio is 2 tablespoons of coffee to 6 ounces of water. After brewing, place coffee in an insulated carafe (to "preheat" your container, fill with very hot water and cover; remove water just before adding coffee).

When entertaining, pamper coffee aficionados with a selection of flavorings and toppings to accompany their favorite brew! Some suggestions:

- Gourmet coffee syrups: hazelnut, caramel, amaretto, vanilla
- Spirited liqueurs: Irish cream, Kahlúa, crème de cacao, crème de cassis
- Sweetened whipped cream (spoon into a chilled bowl, then place in a larger bowl filled with ice)
- Chocolate shavings
- Freshly grated nutmeg
- Cinnamon sticks

In the Wink of an Eye

The Christmas season is such a whirlwind of activity that there never seems to be enough time to just enjoy the company of friends and family. With these make-ahead dishes (and a little bit of prep time), you can be ready to serve drop-in guests in the wink of an eye! We've included appetizers, entrées, and desserts, along with handy tips for stocking your pantry — all to help you have an enjoyable, stress-free holiday!

CHUNKY HAM POT PIE

Feed a hungry throng with this pot pie brimming with ham, veggies, and Cheddar cheese.

  2 **tablespoons butter or margarine**
  1 **cup chopped onion**
  1 **package (10 ounces) frozen broccoli flowerets**
  1 **pound unpeeled red potatoes, coarsely chopped**
  1 **can (10¾ ounces) cream of potato soup, undiluted**
  1 **container (8 ounces) sour cream**
  1 **cup (4 ounces) shredded sharp Cheddar cheese**
  ¾ **cup milk**
  ½ **teaspoon garlic powder**
  ½ **teaspoon salt**
  ¼ **teaspoon pepper**
2½ **cups chopped honey-baked ham or other ham**
  ½ **package (15 ounces) refrigerated pie crusts**

In a large skillet, melt butter over medium heat; add onion. Cook 10 minutes or until onion is tender and begins to brown, stirring often.

Satisfy hearty appetites with Chunky Ham Pot Pie … it's delicious after a day spent playing in the snow or searching for the perfect tree! Frozen veggies, canned soup, and refrigerated pie crusts make this one-dish meal especially easy to prepare.

Cook broccoli according to package directions; drain well. Cook potato in boiling water to cover 10 minutes or until barely tender; drain.

In a large bowl, combine soup and next 6 ingredients, stirring well. Stir in onion, broccoli, potato, and ham. Spoon ham mixture into a greased 3½-quart casserole.

Unfold pie crust onto a lightly floured surface and press out fold lines. Roll pastry to extend ¾ inch beyond edges of casserole. Place pastry over ham mixture. Seal edges and crimp.

TO STORE: Cover and chill casserole overnight.

TO SERVE: Let stand at room temperature 30 minutes. Preheat oven to 400 degrees. Cut slits in top of pastry to allow steam to escape. Bake, uncovered, 45 minutes or until crust is golden brown. Let stand 10 minutes before serving.

Yield: about 6 to 8 servings

Note: You can divide this pot pie into two 2-quart dishes. Bake one for now and freeze one for later. You will need the whole package of pie crusts for 2 casseroles. Top the casserole to be frozen with pastry before freezing, but do not cut slits in top until ready to bake. Let frozen casserole thaw in refrigerator overnight before baking.

People will think you spent hours preparing the rich, sherried sauce for Creamy Beef Stroganoff! To make this meal even quicker, you can pre-cook the noodles, toss with a little olive oil, and store in the refrigerator. To reheat the noodles, put them in a resealable plastic bag and place in a pan of hot (not boiling) water just until heated through.

CREAMY BEEF STROGANOFF

    1   sirloin steak (1½ pounds)
    2   tablespoons vegetable oil
  1½   cups sliced fresh mushrooms
    ½   cup chopped onion
    1   clove garlic, minced
    ½   cup dry sherry
    ½   cup beef broth
    1   tablespoon grated lemon zest
    1   teaspoon dried chervil leaves
    1   teaspoon dried parsley flakes
    ½   teaspoon salt
        Freshly ground pepper
    1   package (3 ounces) cream cheese, cubed
    1   container (8 ounces) sour cream
        Hot cooked noodles
        Additional freshly ground pepper

Partially freeze steak; slice diagonally across grain into ¼-inch strips. In a large skillet, brown meat in hot oil; remove meat, reserving pan drippings in skillet. In reserved pan drippings, sauté mushrooms, onion, and garlic until tender.

Return meat to skillet; add sherry and next 6 ingredients. Cook over medium-low heat 10 to 12 minutes or until most of liquid evaporates. Remove from heat; add cream cheese, stirring until cheese melts. Cool.

TO STORE: Refrigerate meat mixture in a tightly covered container up to 2 days or freeze mixture in an airtight container up to 2 weeks.

TO SERVE: If frozen, thaw in refrigerator. In a large saucepan, cook over medium heat until simmering, stirring frequently. Stir in sour cream; cook just until hot. (Do not boil.) Serve stroganoff over noodles. Sprinkle with additional ground pepper.

Yield: about 4 to 6 servings

TURKEY AND WILD RICE CASSEROLE

- 1 package (6 ounces) long-grain and wild rice mix
- ½ pound bulk pork sausage
- 1 cup sliced fresh mushrooms
- ½ cup sliced celery
- 1 tablespoon cornstarch
- 1 cup milk
- 1 tablespoon Worcestershire sauce
- 3 cups cooked turkey, chopped
- 1 cup sweetened dried cranberries

Prepare rice mix according to package directions. Set aside.

In a large skillet, cook sausage, mushrooms, and celery until sausage is browned, stirring until it crumbles and is no longer pink. Drain sausage mixture, reserving 1 tablespoon drippings in skillet. Set sausage mixture aside.

Add cornstarch to drippings in skillet, stirring until smooth. Cook 1 minute, stirring constantly. Gradually add milk and Worcestershire sauce; cook over medium heat, stirring constantly, until mixture is thickened.

Combine rice, sausage mixture, sauce, turkey, and cranberries. Spoon mixture into a lightly greased 7 x 11-inch baking dish.

TO STORE: Cover and refrigerate up to 2 days or cover tightly and freeze up to 2 weeks.

TO SERVE: If frozen, thaw in refrigerator. Preheat oven to 375 degrees. Bake, uncovered, 40 to 45 minutes.

Yield: about 6 to 8 servings

SMOKY CHEESE BALL

- 1 package (8 ounces) cream cheese, softened
- 1 cup (4 ounces) shredded sharp Cheddar cheese
- 1 cup (4 ounces) shredded smoked Cheddar cheese
- 2 tablespoons milk
- 2 teaspoons Dijon mustard
- ½ cup chopped pecans, toasted
- ¼ cup minced fresh parsley
  Assorted crackers or party pumpernickel bread to serve

In a medium mixing bowl, combine first 5 ingredients; beat at medium speed of an electric mixer until smooth. Cover and chill at least 3 hours. Shape mixture into a ball. Combine pecans and parsley; roll cheese ball in pecan mixture.

TO STORE: Refrigerate in a tightly covered container up to 1 week.

TO SERVE: Let stand at room temperature 30 minutes before serving. Serve with crackers or pumpernickel bread.

Yield: one 3½-inch cheese ball

SALMON TARTS

- 4 refrigerated pie crusts (9 inches each)
- 1½ cups half and half
- 4 large eggs, beaten
- ¼ pound smoked salmon, chopped
- ½ cup (2 ounces) shredded Monterey Jack cheese
- ¼ cup minced green onions
- ½ teaspoon dried dill weed
- ¼ teaspoon salt
- ⅛ teaspoon pepper

Cut each pie crust into 14 circles, using a 2½-inch round cutter. Place rounds in greased miniature muffin cups; trim excess pastry.

In a medium bowl, combine half and half and eggs; whisk until well blended. Stir in salmon and remaining ingredients.

Preheat oven to 375 degrees. Spoon 1 tablespoon salmon mixture into each pastry shell. Bake 25 to 30 minutes or until mixture is set. Remove from pans; cool on wire racks.

TO STORE: Freeze tarts in an airtight container up to 2 weeks.

TO SERVE: Thaw at room temperature. Preheat oven to 375 degrees. Place on baking sheets; cover and bake 5 to 10 minutes or until hot.

Yield: about 4 dozen tarts

CRUNCHY CHEESE SNACKS

- 1 cup (4 ounces) shredded Cheddar cheese
- ¾ cup all-purpose flour
- ¾ cup coarsely crushed crisp rice cereal
- 6 slices bacon, cooked and crumbled
- ¼ teaspoon salt
- ¼ teaspoon dry mustard
- ⅛ teaspoon garlic powder
- ⅛ teaspoon crushed red pepper flakes
- ⅓ cup butter or margarine, softened
- 2 tablespoons cold water
- 24 pecan halves

In a large bowl, combine first 8 ingredients, stirring well. Add butter; stir with a fork until blended. Sprinkle water evenly over surface; stir with a fork until dough forms a ball.

Preheat oven to 350 degrees. Drop dough by level tablespoonfuls onto greased baking sheets. Press a pecan half into center of each cheese snack. Bake 15 to 18 minutes or until lightly browned. Cool on wire racks.

TO STORE: Freeze snacks in an airtight container up to 3 months.

TO SERVE: Thaw at room temperature.

Yield: about 2 dozen cheese snacks

LEMON-CREAM CHEESE SQUARES

⅓ cup butter or margarine, softened
⅓ cup firmly packed brown sugar
1 cup all-purpose flour
½ cup finely chopped pecans
1 package (8 ounces) cream cheese, softened
½ cup granulated sugar
1 large egg
1 teaspoon grated lemon zest
3 tablespoons lemon juice
2 tablespoons milk
½ teaspoon vanilla extract

Preheat oven to 350 degrees. In a mixing bowl, beat butter at medium speed of an electric mixer until creamy; gradually add brown sugar. Gradually add flour, mixing well. Stir in pecans. Reserve ¾ cup crumb mixture. Press remaining crumb mixture in bottom of an ungreased 8-inch square baking pan. Bake 12 to 15 minutes.

In a mixing bowl, beat cream cheese and remaining ingredients at medium speed until creamy. Pour cream cheese mixture over prepared crust; sprinkle with reserved crumb mixture. Bake 25 to 30 minutes or until golden. Cool.
TO STORE: Cover and refrigerate up to 5 days or cover tightly and freeze up to 1 month.
TO SERVE: If frozen, thaw at room temperature. Cut into squares.
Yield: about 16 squares

SOUR CREAM-STREUSEL POUND CAKE

½ cup firmly packed brown sugar
¼ cup chopped pecans
2 tablespoons butter or margarine, softened
2 tablespoons all-purpose flour
1 teaspoon ground cinnamon
1 cup butter or margarine, softened
3 cups granulated sugar
6 large eggs
3 cups all-purpose flour
¼ teaspoon baking powder
¼ teaspoon baking soda
¼ teaspoon salt
1 container (8 ounces) sour cream
2 teaspoons vanilla extract
Confectioners sugar

Combine first 5 ingredients, stirring well. Set aside.
In a large mixing bowl, beat 1 cup butter at medium speed of an electric mixer until creamy; gradually add 3 cups sugar, beating well. Add eggs, 1 at a time, beating after each addition.

Combine 3 cups flour, baking powder, baking soda, and salt; add to butter mixture alternately with sour cream, beginning and ending with flour mixture. Mix just until blended after each addition. Stir in vanilla.

Preheat oven to 325 degrees. Pour half of batter into a greased and floured 12-cup fluted tube pan. Sprinkle pecan mixture over batter; pour remaining batter over pecan mixture. Bake 1¼ hours or until a toothpick inserted in center of cake comes out clean. Cool in pan 10 minutes; remove from pan and cool completely on a wire rack.
TO STORE: Cover and store at room temperature up to 3 days or cover tightly and freeze up to 1 month.
TO SERVE: If frozen, thaw at room temperature. Sift confectioners sugar over cake.
Yield: about 16 servings

Last-Minute Entertaining Tips for the Holidays

If you're short on time during the holidays, here's a handy list of sweet and savory ideas. No recipes needed!

For dressed-up desserts in no time, all you need is:
• Frozen or store-bought pound cake
• Refrigerated sliceable cookie dough
• Brownie mix, cake mix, or pudding mix
• Maraschino cherries with stems
• Ice cream or yogurt
• Frozen whipped topping
• Flavored syrups or ice-cream toppings
• Toasted nuts and flaked coconut
• Candy bars or holiday candies such as peppermint sticks
• Chopped fresh fruit or dried fruit

For drop-in guests to enjoy, keep handy:
• Black, green, or kalamata olives
• Grissini (skinny breadsticks)
• Herb-flavored cheese
• Cream cheese and toppings, such as preserves or pepper jelly or mint jelly, and specialty crackers
• Fruited cream cheese, gingersnaps, and seasonal fruit
• Lemon curd to serve spooned over store-bought pound cake or angel food cake
• Flavored tea bags, coffees, and hot cocoa with mini marshmallows

CHOCOLATE-PECAN TASSIES

½ **cup butter or margarine, softened**
1 **package (3 ounces) cream cheese, softened**
1½ **cups all-purpose flour**
¼ **cup plus 2 tablespoons granulated sugar**
3 **tablespoons cocoa**
1 **cup firmly packed brown sugar**
2 **tablespoons butter or margarine, softened**
2 **large eggs**
¾ **cup chopped pecans**
½ **cup semisweet chocolate chips, coarsely chopped**
2 **teaspoons vanilla extract**

Combine ½ cup butter and cream cheese; stir well. Combine flour, sugar, and cocoa; add to butter mixture, stirring well. Cover and refrigerate 1 hour.

Shape dough into 36 (1-inch) balls. Place in ungreased miniature muffin pans, shaping each ball into a shell.

Preheat oven to 325 degrees. In a mixing bowl, combine brown sugar and 2 tablespoons butter; beat at medium speed until creamy. Add eggs, mixing well. Stir in pecans, chocolate chips, and vanilla. Spoon mixture into pastry shells, filling three-fourths full. Bake 25 to 30 minutes or until lightly browned. Cool in pans 10 minutes. Remove from pans and cool completely on wire racks.

TO STORE: Refrigerate in a tightly covered container up to 2 days or freeze in an airtight container up to 2 weeks.

TO SERVE: If frozen, thaw at room temperature.

Yield: about 3 dozen pastries

From their chocolate pastry crusts to their rich cream-cheese fillings, these tiny Chocolate-Pecan Tassies are packed with flavor! They're delicious with hot coffee or cocoa.

Family Night

Make decorating for the holidays an event the whole family can enjoy! Play your favorite Christmas music while you trim the tree and deck the halls, then settle in with big bowls of steaming gumbo and watch classic holiday movies. After dinner, everyone will enjoy nibbling moist, chewy Blonde Brownies with Chocolate Chunks and sipping Hot Cider Nog. What a great family tradition!

CHICKEN-ANDOUILLE GUMBO

    1 gallon water
    1 chicken (4 pounds)
    5 bay leaves
    5 parsley sprigs
    3 cloves garlic, halved
    1 pound andouille or smoked sausage, sliced
   ¾ cup vegetable oil
    1 cup all-purpose flour
    2 medium onions, chopped
    2 large ribs celery, chopped
    1 large green pepper, chopped
    3 tablespoons minced garlic
    4 chicken bouillon cubes
    1 teaspoon ground red pepper
    1 teaspoon ground black pepper
    1 bunch green onions, chopped
   ½ cup chopped fresh parsley
    1 teaspoon salt
   ½ teaspoon filé powder (optional)
       Hot cooked rice
       Hot sauce (optional)
       Garnish: chopped green onions

In a large stockpot, bring first 5 ingredients to a boil; cover, reduce heat, and simmer 1 hour.

Meanwhile, in a large skillet, brown sausage; drain on paper towels. Set aside.

In a large heavy skillet or Dutch oven, heat oil over medium-low heat; gradually whisk in flour and cook, whisking constantly, until roux is dark (chocolate colored), about 20 to 30 minutes. Remove from heat; add onion, celery, green pepper, and garlic. Cook over medium heat, stirring constantly, 8 to 10 minutes or until vegetables are tender. Remove from heat.

When chicken finishes simmering, remove chicken from broth to cool, reserving broth. Pour broth through a wire-mesh strainer into a large bowl, discarding solids. Skim fat from top of broth. Return broth to stockpot. Add water, if necessary, to measure 1 gallon.

Add roux with vegetables to broth in stockpot. Stir in sausage, bouillon cubes, and ground peppers. Simmer, uncovered, 1½ hours, skimming fat as needed. Meanwhile, skin, bone, and coarsely chop chicken. Add chicken; simmer 45 minutes.

Stir green onions, parsley, and salt into gumbo. Simmer for 5 minutes, stirring occasionally.

Remove gumbo from heat and stir in filé powder, if desired. Serve gumbo over rice with hot sauce, if desired. Garnish with green onions.

Yield: about 14 cups gumbo

PECAN CORNBREAD LOAF

   1½ cups yellow cornmeal
    1 cup all-purpose flour
    1 tablespoon baking powder
    1 teaspoon salt
   ¼ cup sugar
   1½ cups half and half
   ¾ cup butter or margarine, melted
    2 large eggs, lightly beaten
   ½ cup chopped pecans

Preheat oven to 375 degrees. In a large bowl, combine first 5 ingredients; make a well in center of mixture. Set aside.

Combine half and half, butter, eggs, and pecans. Add to dry ingredients; stir just until moistened. Pour batter into a well-greased 5 x 9-inch loaf pan.

Bake 50 to 55 minutes or until golden brown. Remove from pan and serve immediately or cool on a wire rack.

Yield: 1 loaf

A rich, dark roux and a sprinkling of filé powder are the secrets to flavoring Chicken-Andouille Gumbo. Serve the stew with thick slices of warm Pecan Cornbread Loaf for a satisfying meal.

Drizzle a selection of Mixed Greens with a tangy Dijon dressing and team with flavorful Roquefort Firecrackers, a light complement to the hearty gumbo.

MIXED GREENS WITH DIJON DRESSING

DIJON DRESSING

- ½ cup olive oil
- ½ cup vegetable oil
- ½ cup freshly squeezed lemon juice
- 2 tablespoons Dijon mustard
- 3 cloves garlic, pressed
- ¾ teaspoon salt
- ¾ teaspoon pepper

For Dijon dressing, combine all ingredients in a jar. Cover tightly and shake vigorously.

MIXED GREENS

- 2 packages (10 ounces each) gourmet mixed salad greens
- 1 small purple onion, halved and sliced
- 1 can (2¼ ounces) sliced ripe olives

For mixed greens, arrange ingredients on individual salad plates. Drizzle with Dijon dressing; serve with Roquefort Firecrackers.
Yield: about 8 servings

ROQUEFORT FIRECRACKERS

- 4 ounces Roquefort cheese, crumbled
- 1 package (3 ounces) cream cheese, softened
- 8 frozen phyllo pastry sheets, thawed
- ¼ cup butter or margarine, melted
- 16 fresh chives (optional)

Preheat oven to 375 degrees. Combine cheeses, stirring until well blended.

Brush half of 1 phyllo sheet with butter; fold in half. Repeat procedure twice to make a 4 x 6-inch rectangle. Spread 1 rounded tablespoon cheese in center of rectangle. Roll up, jellyroll fashion, starting at long end. Twist ends and place on a lightly greased baking sheet. Repeat procedure with remaining phyllo sheets and cheese.

Bake 10 to 12 minutes or until golden. Tie ends with chives, if desired. Serve immediately.
Yield: 8 firecrackers

BLONDE BROWNIES WITH CHOCOLATE CHUNKS

1 vanilla-flavored baking bar
  (6 ounces)
⅓ cup butter or margarine
2 large eggs, beaten
½ cup sugar
¼ teaspoon vanilla extract
1½ cups all-purpose flour
½ teaspoon baking powder
¼ teaspoon salt
⅔ cup chopped pecans
⅔ cup semisweet chocolate chunks

In a heavy saucepan, combine baking bar and butter; cook over low heat until melted. Set aside to cool slightly.

Preheat oven to 350 degrees. In a large bowl, combine eggs, sugar, and vanilla, stirring until blended. Add butter mixture, mixing well.

Combine flour, baking powder, and salt; stir into butter mixture. Fold in pecans and chocolate. Spoon batter into a greased 9-inch square pan. Bake 25 to 30 minutes. Cool and cut into 1½-inch squares.
Yield: about 3 dozen brownies

HOT CIDER NOG

4 cups half and half
2 cups milk
2 cups apple cider
4 large eggs
1 cup sugar
½ teaspoon ground cinnamon
¼ teaspoon ground nutmeg
⅛ teaspoon salt
1 cup bourbon (optional)
1 cup whipping cream, whipped
  Garnish: cinnamon sticks and
    ground cinnamon

In a large heavy saucepan, whisk together first 8 ingredients; cook over medium-low heat, whisking occasionally, until mixture thickens and coats a spoon (about 15 minutes). Stir in bourbon, if desired. Top each serving with whipped cream. Garnish with cinnamon sticks and ground cinnamon.
Yield: about 5½ cups cider nog

No one can resist these yummy Blonde Brownies with Chocolate Chunks! Use pure apple cider to make the rich, creamy Hot Cider Nog extra special — and be sure to make some without the bourbon for the kids!

A Sweet Sampling

Kick off the holidays by inviting friends over for an evening of delicious indulgence, where desserts aren't the finale … they're the main event! This menu highlights a variety of luscious treats, plus helpful hints for planning a dessert party. Between the moist Crème de Menthe Bars, decadent Chocolate Espresso Cheesecake, and other delicacies, guests will want to sample them all!

CARROT-PRALINE CAKE

Buttery bits of homemade pecan praline punctuate each layer of this stunning carrot cake.

CAKE

- 1 tablespoon butter
- 3 tablespoons granulated sugar
- ½ cup chopped pecans
- 1¼ cups granulated sugar
- ¾ cup vegetable oil
- 1 teaspoon vanilla extract
- 3 large eggs
- 2 cups all-purpose flour
- 1¼ teaspoons baking soda
- ¼ teaspoon salt
- ½ teaspoon ground cinnamon
- 1 can (8 ounces) crushed pineapple in juice, undrained
- 2 cups shredded carrot

FROSTING

- 1 package (8 ounces) cream cheese, softened
- ¼ cup butter, softened
- ¼ cup firmly packed brown sugar
- 1 teaspoon vanilla extract
- 3 cups sifted confectioners sugar
- 1 cup chopped pecans
- 1 can (8 ounces) pineapple tidbits in syrup, drained
- Garnish: pecan halves

What a showstopper! Serve this beautiful candy-studded Carrot-Praline Cake on your best silver platter … and make an extra batch of the pecan pralines for nibbling.

For cake, melt butter in a skillet; add 3 tablespoons sugar and cook over low heat until mixture bubbles. Stir in pecans; cook until pecans are coated and sugar begins to caramelize. Pour onto a sheet of waxed paper; cool. Break pralines into small pieces.

Preheat oven to 350 degrees. In a mixing bowl, beat 1¼ cups sugar, oil, and vanilla at medium speed of an electric mixer 1 minute. Add eggs, 1 at a time; beat until blended after each addition. Combine flour and next 3 ingredients; add to oil mixture, beating at low speed until blended. Stir in pineapple, carrot, and praline pieces. Pour into 2 greased and floured 9-inch round cake pans. Bake 30 minutes or until a toothpick inserted in center of cake comes out clean. Cool in pans on wire racks 10 minutes. Remove from pans; cool completely on wire racks.

For frosting, beat cream cheese and butter in a mixing bowl at medium speed until creamy; gradually add brown sugar and vanilla, beating well. Add confectioners sugar, ½ cup at a time, beating well after each addition. Spread frosting between layers and on top and sides of cake. Press chopped pecans into frosting on sides of cake. Press pineapple into frosting around top edge of cake. Garnish with pecan halves.

Yield: about 12 to 14 servings

CINNAMON-ALMOND-PECAN PIE

- ½ **package (15 ounces) refrigerated pie crusts**
- ⅔ **cup sugar**
- 2 **to 3 teaspoons ground cinnamon**
- 4 **large eggs, lightly beaten**
- 1 **cup light corn syrup**
- 2 **tablespoons butter or margarine, melted**
- 1 **tablespoon vanilla extract**
- 1 **to 1½ teaspoons almond extract**
- 1 **cup coarsely chopped pecans**
- ½ **cup slivered almonds**
- 1 **large egg white, lightly beaten (optional)**

Unfold pie crust and press out fold lines; fit into a 9-inch pie plate; trim excess pastry even with pie plate.

Preheat oven to 350 degrees. In a medium bowl, stir together sugar and next 6 ingredients until blended. Stir in pecans and almonds.

Pour filling into pie crust. Brush edges of pie crust with beaten egg white, if desired.

Bake 40 minutes or until set, covering edges with strips of aluminum foil after 25 minutes to prevent excessive browning.

Yield: about 8 servings

Note: You may use a whole package of pie crusts, cutting shapes from remaining pastry with a cookie cutter and attaching with egg white to edges of crust in pie plate after filling and before baking. We used a holly leaf-shaped cookie cutter.

A wreath of cutout holly leaves adds a festive look to sweet Cinnamon-Almond-Pecan Pie, a flavorful variation of a Southern favorite.

The incredibly delicious flavor and smooth texture of this Chocolate Espresso Cheesecake are worth a bit of extra preparation time. Curls of rich, dark chocolate are the perfect garnish.

CHOCOLATE ESPRESSO CHEESECAKE

2½ cups graham cracker crumbs
½ cup plus 2 tablespoons butter or margarine, melted
2 teaspoons almond extract
4 packages (8 ounces each) cream cheese, softened
⅔ cup sugar
3 large eggs
8 squares (1 ounce each) semisweet chocolate, melted
⅓ cup milk
2 teaspoons instant espresso powder
Garnish: chocolate curls

In a medium bowl, combine first 3 ingredients; stir well. Press mixture on bottom and 2 inches up sides of a 9-inch springform pan. Set aside.

Preheat oven to 350 degrees. In a mixing bowl, beat cream cheese at high speed of an electric mixer until creamy. Gradually add sugar, beating well. Add eggs, 1 at a time, beating after each addition. Add melted chocolate; beat well. Combine milk and espresso powder, stirring until powder dissolves. Add to cream cheese mixture; beat until smooth. Pour mixture into prepared crust.

Bake 45 to 50 minutes or until center is almost set. Let cool to room temperature in pan on a wire rack; cover and chill 8 hours. Carefully remove sides of springform pan. Garnish with chocolate curls.
Yield: about 12 servings

Spiked with brandy and liqueur, Holiday Irish Coffee Eggnog is a creamy complement to our desserts. Other party-time favorites include sesame-sprinkled Caraway Seed Wafers, layered Crème de Menthe Bars, and Spicy Ginger Cookies, which have a surprisingly refreshing flavor.

SPICY GINGER COOKIES

  1 **cup (4 ounces) shredded white Cheddar cheese**
  ½ **cup butter, softened**
  ¾ **teaspoon salt**
  ¼ **to ½ teaspoon ground red pepper**
  1 **cup all-purpose flour**
  2 **teaspoons crystallized ginger, finely chopped**

In a mixing bowl, beat first 4 ingredients at medium speed of an electric mixer until creamy; add flour and mix thoroughly. Shape dough into a ball. Wrap in plastic wrap and chill 30 minutes.

Preheat oven to 350 degrees. Shape dough into 30 balls. Place 1 piece of ginger in center of each ball; place 2 inches apart on ungreased baking sheets and flatten slightly with palm of hand. Bake 15 minutes or until golden brown. Transfer to wire racks to cool.
Yield: about 2½ dozen cookies

HOT MULLED FRUIT CIDER

Take the chill off a winter day by sipping a mug of this mulled cider. It'll warm your spirit and add a welcoming scent throughout your house.

  10 **cinnamon sticks (3 inches each)**
  20 **whole cloves**
  20 **whole allspice**
   8 **cups apple juice**
   4 **cups cranberry juice**
   4 **cups pineapple juice**
   4 **cups water**
  ¼ **cup lemon juice**

Place first 3 ingredients in a cheesecloth bag. In a large Dutch oven, combine juices, water, and spice bag. Bring to a boil and cook 1 minute. Reduce heat and simmer, uncovered, 45 minutes. Remove and discard spice bag. Serve cider warm.
Yield: about 14½ cups cider

CRÈME DE MENTHE BARS

Rich, moist, and luscious layers flavored with chocolate syrup and mint inspired our Test Kitchen staff to give these bars our highest rating.

- ½ cup butter or margarine, softened
- 1 cup granulated sugar
- 4 large eggs
- 1 teaspoon vanilla extract
- 1 cup all-purpose flour
- ½ teaspoon salt
- 1 can (16 ounces) chocolate syrup
- ½ cup chopped pecans
- ½ cup butter or margarine, softened
- 2 cups sifted confectioners sugar
- 1½ tablespoons crème de menthe
- 1 cup (6 ounces) semisweet chocolate chips
- 6 tablespoons butter or margarine

In a mixing bowl, beat ½ cup butter at medium speed of an electric mixer until creamy; add granulated sugar, beating well. Add eggs and vanilla; beat well.

Preheat oven to 350 degrees. Combine flour and salt; add to butter mixture, beating well. Stir in chocolate syrup and pecans. Pour batter into a greased 9 x 13-inch pan. Bake 30 minutes. Cool completely in pan on a wire rack.

In a mixing bowl, beat ½ cup butter at medium speed until creamy; add confectioners sugar and crème de menthe, beating until smooth. Spread over cooled brownie layer.

In a heavy saucepan, combine chocolate chips and 6 tablespoons butter over low heat, stirring until smooth. Cool 5 minutes and spread over crème de menthe layer. Cover and chill at least 1 hour. Cut into bars.

Yield: about 2 dozen bars

CARAWAY SEED WAFERS

Anise-flavored caraway seeds and only a hint of sweetness flavor these tender cookies, making them the perfect accompaniment to this dessert party menu.

- 1½ cups all-purpose flour
- 1½ teaspoons baking powder
- ½ teaspoon salt
- ½ teaspoon ground nutmeg
- 1 large egg
- ½ cup firmly packed brown sugar
- ½ cup heavy whipping cream
- 2 teaspoons caraway seeds
  Sesame seeds (optional)

In a medium bowl, combine first 4 ingredients. In a large mixing bowl, beat egg at medium speed of an electric mixer. Gradually add brown sugar and cream to egg, beating well. Stir in flour mixture and caraway seeds. Cover and chill overnight.

Preheat oven to 350 degrees. Divide dough in half. Work with 1 portion of dough at a time, storing remaining dough in refrigerator. Roll each portion of dough to ⅛-inch thickness on a heavily floured surface. Cut with a 3-inch cookie cutter and place cookies on lightly greased baking sheets. Sprinkle with sesame seeds, if desired.

Bake 10 minutes or until lightly browned. Cool slightly on baking sheets; remove to wire racks to cool completely.

Yield: about 2 dozen wafers

HOLIDAY IRISH COFFEE EGGNOG

Cheers to this holiday nog! Adding hot brewed coffee and a couple of choice spirits elevates this favorite beverage to a new level.

- 2½ cups hot brewed coffee
- 1 cup sugar
- 2 quarts refrigerated eggnog
- 1⅓ cups Irish cream liqueur
- 1 cup brandy

Combine coffee and sugar, stirring until sugar dissolves. Stir in eggnog, liqueur, and brandy. Cover eggnog and chill thoroughly.

Yield: about 14 cups eggnog

Note: Eggnog can be made up to 3 days ahead.

Dessert Planning Guidelines

When hosting a dessert party, count on cakes and pies serving twice the number of typical servings, because guests prefer smaller portions in order to sample everything. The desserts featured in this menu will amply serve 20 to 24 guests. Also plan on a couple of nonsweet or less-sweet items to serve. We included Spicy Ginger Cookies and Caraway Seed Wafers to accompany this dessert menu. And don't forget to offer a nonalcoholic beverage to serve as well. Guests will love the warmth of the Hot Mulled Fruit Cider, as well as the spirits in the Holiday Irish Coffee Eggnog. With the exception of the hot cider, all the recipes can be made a day or 2 in advance, allowing you more time with your guests.

Baker's Dozen

If sweet confections are your fancy, you won't be able to resist this "baker's dozen"! Our sampling of cookies and candies features thirteen enticing temptations, including chocolaty macaroons, giant sorghum cookies, nutty chocolate-coated toffee, and other delectable treats. They're too good to keep to yourself, so make plenty to share with friends … and some to leave out for old Saint Nick, too!

APRICOT JEWEL COOKIES

COOKIES

- 1¼ cups all-purpose flour
- 1½ teaspoons baking powder
- ¼ teaspoon salt
- ¼ cup sugar
- ½ cup butter or margarine, softened
- 1 package (3 ounces) cream cheese, softened
- ½ cup flaked coconut
- ½ cup chopped pecans
- ½ cup apricot preserves

FROSTING

- 1 cup sifted confectioners sugar
- ¼ cup apricot preserves
- 1 teaspoon butter or margarine, melted
- ¼ cup finely chopped pecans, toasted (optional)

For cookies, preheat oven to 350 degrees. In a large bowl, combine first 4 ingredients. Using a pastry blender or 2 knives, cut in butter and cream cheese until mixture is crumbly. Add coconut, ½ cup pecans, and preserves; stir well.

Drop dough by heaping teaspoonfuls onto greased baking sheets. Bake 8 to 10 minutes or until lightly browned. Transfer to wire racks to cool slightly.

For frosting, combine all ingredients; stir well. Spread warm cookies with frosting. Sprinkle with toasted pecans, if desired.

Yield: about 4 dozen cookies

A sprinkling of toasted pecans enhances the fruity goodness of frosted Apricot Jewel Cookies (on plate). Chewy Chocolate Macaroons (recipe on page 100) and pretty Chocolate-Cherry Swirls are sure to become cookie jar favorites.

CHOCOLATE-CHERRY SWIRLS

- 1 cup butter, softened
- 1 cup sugar
- 1 large egg
- 1 teaspoon vanilla extract
- 3 cups all-purpose flour
- 1½ teaspoons baking powder
- ¼ teaspoon salt
- ½ cup drained, minced maraschino cherries
- 3 tablespoons all-purpose flour
- 2 squares (1 ounce each) semisweet chocolate, melted and cooled

In a mixing bowl, beat butter at medium speed of an electric mixer until creamy; gradually add sugar, beating well. Add egg and vanilla; beat well.

Combine flour, baking powder, and salt; stir well. Add flour mixture to butter mixture, beating at low speed.

Remove half of dough from bowl. Add cherries to dough in bowl and mix well. If dough is too soft, add 3 tablespoons flour. Remove cherry dough from mixing bowl. Set aside. Return plain dough to mixing bowl; add chocolate, beating well. Cover and chill both portions of dough 1 hour.

Roll each half of dough into an 8 x 15-inch rectangle on floured waxed paper. Place cherry dough on top of chocolate dough; peel off top waxed paper. Tightly roll dough, jellyroll fashion, starting at short side and peeling remaining waxed paper from dough while rolling. Cover and chill 1 hour.

Preheat oven to 350 degrees. Slice dough into ¼-inch-thick slices; place on ungreased baking sheets. Bake 10 to 12 minutes. Transfer to wire racks to cool.

Yield: about 2½ dozen cookies

Note: To prevent flat-sided cookies, turn dough rolls halfway through the second chilling time. Dental floss makes cutting the dough easier.

CHOCOLATE MACAROONS

Two favorites — chocolate and coconut — come together in these cookies that'll have you raving.

- **1 cup (6 ounces) semisweet chocolate chips**
- **1 cup flaked coconut**
- **½ cup finely chopped walnuts**
- **2 egg whites**
- **¼ teaspoon salt**
- **½ cup sugar**

Place chocolate chips in a microwave-safe bowl. Microwave on high power (100%) 1 to 1½ minutes; stir until smooth. Stir in coconut and walnuts. Let cool to room temperature.

Preheat oven to 350 degrees. In a mixing bowl, beat egg whites and salt at high speed of an electric mixer until foamy. Gradually add sugar, 1 tablespoon at a time, beating until stiff peaks form and sugar dissolves (2 to 4 minutes). Fold egg white mixture into chocolate mixture.

Drop by heaping teaspoonfuls onto baking sheets lined with aluminum foil. Bake 12 minutes. Transfer cookies to wire racks to cool completely.

Yield: about 3 dozen cookies

POUND CAKE COOKIES

Once you taste these buttery gems, you'll agree that they're a hands-down winner for any occasion.

- **1 cup butter, softened**
- **1 cup sugar**
- **1 egg yolk**
- **1 teaspoon rum OR ½ teaspoon imitation rum flavoring**
- **½ teaspoon vanilla extract**
- **2¼ cups sifted cake flour**
- **½ teaspoon salt**
- **About 42 pecan halves**

In a mixing bowl, beat butter at medium speed of an electric mixer until creamy; gradually add sugar, beating well. Add egg yolk, rum, and vanilla; beat well.

In a mixing bowl, combine flour and salt; gradually add to butter mixture, beating well. Cover and

When neighbors drop in for coffee, set out a tray of buttery Pound Cake Cookies and Magic Peanut Butter Middles ... your house will be the most popular destination on the block!

chill at least 2 hours or until firm.

Preheat oven to 350 degrees. Shape dough into 1-inch balls; place 2 inches apart on ungreased baking sheets. Press 1 pecan half into each cookie.

Bake 12 to 14 minutes or until edges are lightly browned. Cool 2 minutes on baking sheets; transfer cookies to wire racks to cool completely.

Yield: about 3½ dozen cookies

MAGIC PEANUT BUTTER MIDDLES

Creamy peanut butter awaits in each bite of these chewy chocolate cookies.

- **½ cup butter or margarine, softened**
- **1 cup creamy peanut butter, divided**
- **½ cup granulated sugar**
- **½ cup firmly packed brown sugar**
- **1 large egg**
- **1 teaspoon vanilla extract**
- **1½ cups all-purpose flour**
- **½ teaspoon baking soda**
- **½ cup cocoa**
- **¾ cup sifted confectioners sugar**
- **Granulated sugar**

In a mixing bowl, beat butter and ¼ cup peanut butter at medium speed of an electric mixer until creamy; gradually add granulated sugar and brown sugar, beating well. Add egg and vanilla; beat well. Combine flour, baking soda, and cocoa; gradually add to butter mixture, beating well. Set aside.

Combine remaining ¾ cup peanut butter and confectioners sugar, beating until blended. With floured hands, shape mixture into 30 (1-inch) balls.

Preheat oven to 300 degrees. Shape about 1 tablespoon chocolate mixture around each peanut butter ball. Place 2 inches apart on ungreased baking sheets. Dip a flat-bottomed glass into granulated sugar and flatten each ball into a 1½-inch circle. Bake 10 to 12 minutes (cookies will be soft). Cool slightly on baking sheets; transfer to wire racks to cool completely.

Yield: about 2½ dozen cookies

CINNAMON-SUGAR ANGELS

This tender cinnamon dough deserves its celestial shape but works fine with whatever cutters you have on hand.

- ¾ **cup unsalted butter, softened**
- 1 **cup granulated sugar**
- 1 **large egg**
- 1 **teaspoon vanilla extract**
- 3 **cups all-purpose flour**
- 2 **teaspoons baking powder**
- ½ **teaspoon baking soda**
- ½ **teaspoon ground cinnamon**
- ¼ **teaspoon salt**
- 1 **container (15 ounces) creamy vanilla frosting**
- ½ **cup coarse decorating sugar**

In a mixing bowl, beat butter at medium speed of an electric mixer until fluffy; gradually add sugar, beating well. Add egg and vanilla, beating well. Combine flour and next 4 ingredients; gradually add to butter mixture, beating until blended. Shape dough into a ball. Cover and chill 30 minutes.

Preheat oven to 375 degrees. Roll dough to ⅛-inch thickness on a lightly floured surface. Cut with a 3-inch angel-shaped cookie cutter and gently transfer to lightly greased baking sheets (dough is fragile). Bake 6 to 7 minutes or until lightly browned. Carefully transfer cookies to wire racks to cool. Place frosting in a microwave-safe bowl. Microwave, uncovered, at high power (100%) 45 seconds or just until pourable; spoon frosting on top of cookies. Sprinkle with coarse decorating sugar. Let stand on wire racks until dry.

Yield: about 3 dozen cookies

NUTTY FINGERS

These pecan-studded cookies are called fingers because of their slender shape. Rolling the cookies in confectioners sugar makes them all the more dainty.

- ½ **cup plus 2 tablespoons butter or margarine, softened**
- ¾ **cup sifted confectioners sugar, divided**
- 2 **cups all-purpose flour**
- 1 **tablespoon ice water**
- 1 **tablespoon vanilla extract**
- 1 **cup finely chopped pecans**

In a mixing bowl, beat butter at medium speed of an electric mixer until creamy; gradually add ¼ cup confectioners sugar, beating well. Add flour, water, and vanilla, beating well. (Dough will be crumbly.) Stir in pecans.

Preheat oven to 350 degrees. Shape dough into 2 x ½-inch fingers; place on greased baking sheets. Bake 14 to 16 minutes or until lightly browned. Cool completely on wire racks. Roll cookies in remaining ½ cup confectioners sugar.

Yield: about 4 dozen cookies

A dusting of coarse sugar crystals gives Cinnamon-Sugar Angels a celestial sparkle. Pair them with sugar-coated Nutty Fingers for a dainty teatime treat.

CAN'T-FAIL DIVINITY

Marshmallow creme gives this candy a denser texture than regular divinity, and it's oh, so tasty!

- **2 cups sugar**
- **½ cup water**
- **⅛ teaspoon salt**
- **2 jars (7 ounces each) marshmallow creme**
- **1 teaspoon vanilla extract**
- **½ cup chopped pecans, toasted**

In a large heavy saucepan, combine first 3 ingredients; stirring constantly, cook over low heat until sugar dissolves. Using a pastry brush dipped in hot water, wash down any sugar crystals from sides of pan. Attach a candy thermometer to pan, making sure thermometer does not touch bottom of pan. Cook, without stirring, until mixture reaches hard-ball stage (approximately 260 degrees). Remove from heat.

Place marshmallow creme in a large mixing bowl. Pour hot sugar mixture in a heavy stream over marshmallow creme, beating at high speed of a heavy-duty mixer. Add vanilla, beating just until mixture holds its shape (7 to 9 minutes). Stir in pecans.

Working quickly, drop divinity by rounded teaspoonfuls onto waxed paper; let stand until firm.
Yield: about 2½ dozen candies

PECAN TOFFEE

This old-fashioned cooked sugar candy is topped with the goodness of chocolate and nuts. You'll want to make several batches for munching and sharing.

- **1½ cups chopped pecans, divided**
- **1 cup sugar**
- **1 cup butter, softened**
- **⅓ cup water**
- **6 milk chocolate bars (1.55 ounces each), broken into small pieces**

Line a 10½ x 15½-inch jellyroll pan with heavy-duty aluminum foil; lightly grease foil. Sprinkle

A generous portion of marshmallow creme is the secret to making Can't-Fail Divinity, and creamy milk chocolate provides a delightful contrast in irresistible Pecan Toffee.

with 1 cup pecans to within 1 inch of edges.

In a heavy saucepan, bring sugar, butter, and water to a boil over medium heat, stirring constantly. Attach a candy thermometer to pan, making sure thermometer does not touch bottom of pan. Stirring constantly, cook over medium-high heat 12 minutes or until mixture

reaches hard-crack stage (approximately 300 to 310 degrees). Pour over pecans; sprinkle with chocolate pieces. Let stand 30 seconds.

Sprinkle with remaining ½ cup pecans. Chill 30 minutes. Using a meat mallet or rolling pin, break up toffee. Store in an airtight container.
Yield: about 1¾ pounds toffee

Flavored with fruity liqueur and studded with fresh berries, Really Raspberry Brownies are a dream-come-true for chocolate lovers!

REALLY RASPBERRY BROWNIES

- **1 cup unsalted butter, softened**
- **1¼ cups granulated sugar**
- **½ cup firmly packed brown sugar**
- **4 large eggs**
- **1¼ cups all-purpose flour**
- **½ cup cocoa**
- **¼ teaspoon salt**
- **3 tablespoons framboise or other raspberry-flavored liqueur (see note), divided**
- **1 teaspoon vanilla extract**
- **2 cups fresh raspberries**
- **4 squares (1 ounce each) semisweet chocolate**
- **2 teaspoons hot water**
- **Sifted confectioners sugar**

Preheat oven to 325 degrees. In a mixing bowl, beat butter at medium speed of an electric mixer until creamy; gradually add granulated sugar and brown sugar, beating well. Add eggs, 1 at a time, beating well after each addition.

Combine flour, cocoa, and salt; add to butter mixture, beating well. Stir in 1 tablespoon framboise and vanilla. Spoon batter into a greased 9 x 13-inch pan. Sprinkle with raspberries. Bake 40 minutes or until a toothpick inserted in center comes out clean. Let cool completely in pan on a wire rack.

Combine chocolate, remaining 2 tablespoons framboise, and water in top of a double boiler; bring water in bottom of double boiler to a boil. Reduce heat to low; cook until chocolate melts, stirring occasionally. Remove from heat and let cool slightly. Cut brownies into squares. Sprinkle with confectioners sugar.

Place chocolate mixture in a small heavy-duty resealable plastic bag. Snip off 1 corner of bag to create a small opening. Drizzle chocolate mixture over brownies.

Yield: about 2 dozen brownies
Note: Try the Raspberry Cordial, page 18, in this recipe.

GIANT GINGER-OATMEAL SORGHUM COOKIES

    4 cups all-purpose flour
    1 tablespoon baking soda
1½ teaspoons salt
    4 cups quick-cooking oats
1¼ cups granulated sugar
1½ teaspoons ground ginger
1½ cups raisins
    1 cup butter or margarine,
        melted
    1 cup sorghum
    1 cup chopped walnuts
    2 tablespoons hot water
    2 large eggs, lightly beaten
    1 to 2 tablespoons water
    ½ cup coarse decorating sugar

In a large bowl, combine first 7 ingredients; add butter and next 4 ingredients, stirring until blended.

Preheat oven to 375 degrees. Shape dough into 36 (2½-inch) balls. Place 2 inches apart on lightly greased baking sheets; flatten each to ¼-inch thickness. Brush tops with 1 to 2 tablespoons water and sprinkle with coarse decorating sugar.

Bake 8 to 10 minutes or until lightly browned. Transfer to wire racks to cool completely.
Yield: about 3 dozen cookies

CHOCOLATE-DIPPED COFFEE KISSES

    3 egg whites
    ¼ teaspoon cream of tartar
    1 tablespoon instant coffee
        granules
    1 cup sugar
    ½ teaspoon vanilla extract
    ½ cup chopped walnuts
    3 squares (2 ounces each)
        chocolate candy coating,
        melted
    1 cup finely chopped walnuts,
        toasted

Preheat oven to 225 degrees. In a mixing bowl, beat first 3 ingredients at high speed of an electric mixer just until foamy. Add sugar, 1 tablespoon at a time, beating until stiff peaks form. Fold in vanilla and ½ cup

Our old-fashioned Giant Ginger-Oatmeal Sorghum Cookies will be a hit with young and old alike … and Santa, too!

walnuts. Drop by tablespoonfuls onto parchment paper-lined baking sheets.

Bake 1¼ hours. Turn off oven and leave cookies in oven 2 hours.

Dip bottom of each cookie into melted coating and press into toasted walnuts. Place on waxed paper until dry.
Yield: about 3½ dozen cookies

BUTTERMILK PRALINES

½ **cup buttermilk**
½ **teaspoon baking soda**
2 **cups firmly packed light brown sugar**
2 **tablespoons butter or margarine**
2 **tablespoons light corn syrup**
1 **cup chopped pecans, toasted**
1 **teaspoon vanilla extract**

In a large heavy saucepan, stir together buttermilk and baking soda until blended. Add brown sugar, butter, and corn syrup.

Attach a candy thermometer to pan, making sure thermometer does not touch bottom of pan. Cook, stirring constantly, over medium-high heat 8 to 10 minutes or until mixture reaches soft-ball stage (approximately 234 to 240 degrees). Cool 10 to 12 minutes.

Beat with a wooden spoon 4 to 5 minutes or until mixture thickens slightly. Stir in pecans and vanilla. Working rapidly, drop by rounded teaspoonfuls onto lightly greased waxed paper. Let stand until firm.
Yield: about 2 dozen candies

For a flavorful twist on meringue cookies, present a platter of delicate Chocolate-Dipped Coffee Kisses at your next get-together. Southern-style Buttermilk Pralines are packed with luscious toasted pecans.

To: Vickie
From: JoAnne

Tasty Treats to Share

These homemade holiday treats will warm hearts and tickle tummies! Surprise a snacker with a festively decorated jar of sugared pecans or "reindeer gorp," or provide a quick-fix dinner for a busy mom with spicy bean soup mix and a bag of cheesy cornmeal muffin mix. You can't go wrong with any of these edible goodies!

SPICY SOUTHWEST CHILE OIL

Scour antique stores, flea markets, or import stores for decorative bottles, then add chiles for gifts with a kick.

- 4 **cloves garlic**
- 2 **tablespoons white vinegar**
- 1 **jalapeño pepper**
- 1 **tablespoon coriander seeds**
- 2 **teaspoons cumin seeds**
- 2 **teaspoons dried oregano**
- 2 **cups extra virgin olive oil, divided**
- 2 **serrano chile peppers, cut in half**
- 2 **red chile peppers, cut in half**

In a small glass bowl, combine garlic and vinegar; cover and refrigerate at least 8 hours. Drain garlic, discarding vinegar; rinse garlic and pat dry with paper towels. Set garlic aside.

Remove stem from jalapeño pepper. Set pepper aside.

Heat a large skillet over medium heat 2 minutes; add coriander and cumin seeds. Stirring constantly, cook 5 minutes or until lightly browned.

Transfer browned seeds to container of an electric blender; add garlic, jalapeño pepper, oregano, and 1 cup olive oil. Cover and process until minced, stopping once to scrape down sides. Pour mixture into a jar; add remaining 1 cup olive oil. Cover and refrigerate 24 hours.

Let oil stand at room temperature 2 hours. Pour mixture through a wire-mesh strainer lined with 2 layers of cheesecloth, then into a decorative bottle or jar, discarding solids. Add chiles. Seal bottle with a cork or other airtight lid. Store in refrigerator up to 1 month.

Use chile oil in salsas, fajitas, beans, and marinades for fish, or brush on vegetables before roasting.
Yield: about 1½ cups chile oil

Gift Bottle and Tag

You will need jute twine, decorative glass bottle, dried chile peppers, greenery, red and green card stock, decorative-edge craft scissors, craft glue stick, black permanent fine-point marker, and a hot glue gun.

1. Wrap a length of jute around neck of bottle; tie into a square knot and trim ends. Tie a second length of jute into a bow around bottle, tucking ends of chile peppers and greenery under bow.
2. For tag, cut a piece of green card stock; use craft scissors to cut a larger piece of red card stock. Using craft glue stick, center and glue green piece to red piece. Use marker to write message and draw details on tag. Hot glue tag behind jute bow.

SPICY BEAN SOUP MIX

- 1 pound dried black beans
- 1 pound dried great Northern beans
- 1 pound dried navy beans
- 1 pound dried pinto beans
- 1 pound dried red beans
- 1 pound dried black-eyed peas
- 1 pound dried green split peas
- 1 pound dried yellow split peas
- 1 pound dried lentils
- 1 pound dried baby limas
- 1 pound dried large limas
- 1 pound pearl barley

In a very large bowl, combine all ingredients. Divide evenly into 13 (2-cup) resealable plastic bags to give with recipe for Spicy Bean Soup.

Yield: 26 cups mix

SPICY BEAN SOUP

- 1 package (2 cups) Spicy Bean Soup Mix
- 2 quarts water
- 2 ham-flavored bouillon cubes
- 2 cans (10 ounces each) diced tomatoes and green chiles, undrained
- 1 large onion, chopped
- 3 tablespoons lemon juice
- 1 chile pepper, coarsely chopped
- 1 clove garlic, minced
- ½ teaspoon salt
- ¼ teaspoon pepper

Sort and wash soup mix; place in a Dutch oven. Cover with water 2 inches above soup mix; let soak 8 hours.

Drain soup mix and return to Dutch oven; add 2 quarts water and bouillon cubes. Bring to a boil; cover, reduce heat, and simmer 1 hour or until beans are tender.

Stir in tomatoes and green chiles and next 4 ingredients. Bring to a boil; reduce heat and simmer, uncovered, 30 minutes.

Stir in salt and pepper.

Yield: about 3 quarts soup

Note: To speed soaking time, boil 2 quarts water. Add bean mixture and boil 3 minutes. Remove from heat; cover and let stand 1 hour. Drain and proceed as directed.

WINTER WARMER SOUP

Homespun Gift Bags and Recipe Cards

You will need pinking shears, two coordinating fabrics, paper-backed fusible web, burlap, craft glue, buttons, jute twine, corrugated craft cardboard, raffia, and card stock.

1. For each bag, use pinking shears to cut a 6" x 20" piece of fabric. Matching short edges and right sides, fold fabric piece in half; using a ¼" seam allowance and leaving top edge open, sew sides of bag together. Turn bag right side out; press.

2. Cut one 3" x 12½" strip each of fusible web and coordinating fabric. Follow manufacturer's instructions to fuse web to wrong side of fabric; use pinking shears to trim edges, then remove paper backing.

3. Overlapping ends at center back, fuse strip to bag 2" from bottom. Cut a ¼" x 12" strip of burlap; fray edges and glue along center of fused strip. Glue three buttons to strip.

4. Place bag of soup mix in gift bag.

5. Cut two lengths of jute; tie into a bow around top of bag. Glue a button to center of bow.

6. For each card, cut a 4" x 8½" piece of cardboard; cut 3½" and 2½" squares of coordinating fabrics and a 1¼" square of burlap. Matching short edges, fold cardboard in half. Glue 3½" square, 2½" square, then burlap square to center front of card. Thread raffia through holes in button and tie into a bow; glue to center of burlap.

7. Write recipe on a 3½" x 8" piece of card stock; glue to inside of card.

ZESTY LITTLE MUFFINS

CHEESE-AND-PEPPER MUFFIN MIX

2½ cups all-purpose flour
¼ cup yellow cornmeal
¼ cup sugar
1 tablespoon baking powder
1 teaspoon baking soda
¾ teaspoon salt
¼ teaspoon ground red pepper
½ cup grated Parmesan cheese
⅓ cup cultured buttermilk powder
1 tablespoon dried chives
1½ to 2 teaspoons crushed red pepper flakes

In a large bowl, combine all ingredients. Store in a resealable plastic bag in a cool dry place.
Yield: 4 cups muffin mix
To Bake: Preheat oven to 400 degrees. Grease muffin pans. Place muffin mix in a large bowl and make a well in center of mixture. Combine 2 eggs, 1½ cups water, and ¼ cup vegetable oil; add to dry ingredients, stirring just until moistened. Fill muffin cups about two-thirds full. Bake 20 minutes. Remove from pans immediately.
Yield: about 2 dozen muffins

Gift Bag and Recipe Card
You will need a 6" x 20" piece of fabric, natural raffia, hot glue gun, artificial leaves, dried chile peppers, decorative-edge craft scissors, brown card stock, colored pencils, and a black permanent fine-point marker.

1. Fringe short edges of fabric piece ¹/₂". Matching right sides and short edges, fold fabric piece in half; using a ¹/₄" seam allowance and leaving top edges open, sew sides of bag together. Turn bag right side out and press.
2. Place muffin mix in gift bag.
3. Knot lengths of raffia around bag; glue leaves, then peppers to knot.
4. For tag, use craft scissors to cut a 3" x 4" piece of card stock. Embellish with colored pencils and marker; write message on front of tag and baking instructions on back of tag. Tuck corner of card under peppers and leaves; glue in place.

NORTH POLE SNACK MIX

REINDEER GORP

- 1 package (14 ounces) holiday-colored candy-coated chocolate pieces
- 1 jar (12 ounces) salted roasted peanuts
- 1 can (6 ounces) salted natural almonds
- 1 package (6 ounces) semisweet chocolate chips
- 1 cup butterscotch chips
- 1 cup raisins

Combine all ingredients, stirring gently. Store in an airtight container.

Yield: about 2 quarts snack mix

Reindeer Jar

You will need tracing paper; removable tape; glass jar with lid; rubbing alcohol; black fine-point paint pen; paintbrushes; blue, brown, red, green, and yellow acrylic paint; spray primer; red spray paint; wooden star cutout; clear acrylic brush-on sealer; hot glue gun; and ribbon.

Allow alcohol, paint pen, paint, and sealer to dry after each application. More than one coat of paint may be necessary for complete coverage.

1. Wipe outside of jar with alcohol.
2. Trace reindeer pattern, page 115, onto tracing paper. Position and tape pattern inside jar.
3. On outside of jar, use paint pen to paint over outline of reindeer.
4. Paint background around reindeer blue and reindeer brown with a red nose. Paint a green wreath with red berries on reindeer's neck. Paint yellow stars on background. Use paint pen to add hooves and an eye and to outline reindeer again.
5. Spray jar lid with primer, then paint red. Paint wooden star yellow; use marker to personalize star.
6. Apply two coats of sealer to painted area on jar and to lid and star.
7. Glue star to top of lid. Tie a length of ribbon into a bow around neck of jar.

SUGAR–AND–SPICE PECANS

¾ cup sugar
1 teaspoon ground cinnamon
½ teaspoon salt
¼ teaspoon ground nutmeg
¼ teaspoon ground allspice
¼ teaspoon ground cloves
1 egg white
2½ tablespoons water
8 cups pecan halves

Preheat oven to 275 degrees. In a medium bowl, combine first 8 ingredients; stir well. Add pecans; stir until evenly coated. Spread in a lightly greased, aluminum foil-lined 10½ x 15½-inch jellyroll pan. Bake 50 to 55 minutes, stirring occasionally.

Remove from pan and cool on waxed paper. Store pecans in an airtight container.

Yield: about 8 cups pecans

NUTCRACKER TREATS

Nutcracker Canister

You will need tracing paper; decorative glass canister with airtight lid; removable tape; rubbing alcohol; flesh, blue, black, and assorted colors of acrylic paint; paintbrushes; transfer paper; stylus; gold, black, and red paint pens; clear acrylic brush-on sealer; hot glue gun; artificial fur; red and ecru card stock; ¼" dia. hole punch; and narrow ribbon.

Refer to Painting Techniques, page 151, before beginning project. Allow paint and sealer to dry after each application. More than one coat of paint may be necessary for complete coverage.

1. Wipe outside of canister with alcohol; allow to dry.
2. Trace nutcracker pattern, page 116, onto tracing paper. Position pattern inside canister and tape in place.
3. Painting on outside of canister, paint background flesh. Remove pattern and position over painted area on outside of canister; using transfer paper and stylus, transfer facial features to canister. Paint face. Paint a blue shirt and hat and a black collar on nutcracker.
4. Use gold paint pen to paint a sawtooth design for band on hat and braid on jacket. Use black paint pen to outline painted facial features and braid. Apply two coats of sealer to painted areas.
5. Hot glue pieces of fur to canister for hair and beard.
6. For tag, cut a 2½" x 3½" background piece of red card stock; use gold paint pen to paint a sawtooth design along edges of background. Cut a 1½" x 2½" piece of ecru card stock; center and glue to background. Use black paint pen to write name on tag.
7. Punch a hole in tag; use ribbon to attach tag to canister.

HEAVEN-SENT TRUFFLES

CHOCOLATE-PRALINE TRUFFLES

 3 **semisweet chocolate bars (4 ounces each), broken into pieces**
 ¼ **cup plus 2 tablespoons whipping cream, divided**
 3 **tablespoons butter, cut into pieces**
 2 **tablespoons almond liqueur**
 1½ **cups finely chopped pecans**
 ¼ **cup firmly packed light brown sugar**

In a 2-quart microwave-safe bowl, microwave semisweet chocolate and ¼ cup whipping cream at medium power (50%) 3½ minutes.

Whisk until chocolate melts and mixture is smooth. (If chocolate doesn't melt completely, microwave and whisk at 15-second intervals until melted.) Whisk in butter and liqueur; let stand 20 minutes.

In a mixing bowl, beat at medium speed of an electric mixer 4 minutes or until mixture forms soft peaks. (Do not overbeat mixture.) Cover and chill at least 4 hours.

Preheat oven to 350 degrees. In a bowl, stir together pecans, brown sugar, and remaining 2 tablespoons whipping cream; spread into a lightly buttered 9-inch round cake pan.

Bake 20 minutes, stirring once, or until coating appears slightly crystallized. Remove from oven; stir and cool. Store in an airtight container.

Shape chilled chocolate mixture into 1-inch balls; roll in praline pecans. Place in resealable plastic bags and chill up to 1 week, or freeze up to 1 month.
Yield: about 2 dozen truffles

Angelic Tag and Decorative Tin
You will need a round corrugated tin with rusted lid, tissue paper, 1"w ribbon, craft glue, greenery sprigs, card stock, colored pencils, decorative-edge craft scissors, ¼" dia. hole punch, and ¼"w satin ribbon.

1. Line inside of tin with tissue paper; place gift in tin.
2. Tie 1"w ribbon around tin and into a bow at top of tin; glue greenery to lid and allow to dry.
3. For tag, photocopy angel pattern, page 117, onto card stock. Color tag. Use craft scissors to trim tag close to edges of angel. Punch a hole at top of tag; use ribbon to attach tag to tin.

SAUCY TREAT

PRALINE SAUCE

¼ cup butter or margarine
1¼ cups firmly packed light brown sugar
¾ cup light corn syrup
3 tablespoons all-purpose flour
1½ cups chopped pecans, toasted
1 can (5 ounces) evaporated milk

In a medium saucepan, melt butter; add brown sugar, corn syrup, and flour, stirring until smooth. Bring to a boil; reduce heat and simmer, stirring constantly, 5 minutes. Remove from heat and let cool 20 minutes. Stir in pecans and evaporated milk. Cool completely.

Pour into gift jar and refrigerate up to 2 weeks. Serve warm over ice cream, plain cheesecake, or pound cake.

Yield: about 3 cups sauce

"From Our House" Tag and Jar

You will need white and green card stock, colored pencils, black permanent fine-point marker, decorative-edge craft scissors, craft glue stick, ribbon, jar with dark lid, hot glue gun, and a heart-shaped button.

1. For tag, photocopy house design, page 117, onto white card stock. Cut out house just inside outer lines.
2. To make roof, fold top edge of house down (about ³/₄") to just above decorative roofline.
3. Color house. Use marker to write "From Our House to Yours" on roof and "Serve Praline Sauce warm over ice cream or cake." under the roof and add a sentiment.
4. Use craft scissors to cut a 2³/₄" × 3⁵/₈" piece of green card stock for background. Use glue stick to glue house to background.
5. Tie a length of ribbon into a bow around jar of Praline Sauce; hot glue button to bow.
6. Give jar with tag.

SOUR CREAM YEAST ROLLS

¼ cup butter or margarine
½ cup sour cream
¼ cup sugar
½ teaspoon salt
1 package quick-acting dry yeast
¼ cup warm water (100 to 110 degrees)
1 large egg, beaten
2 cups all-purpose flour
Melted butter

In a saucepan, melt butter over low heat. Remove from heat and stir in sour cream, sugar, and salt, stirring until sugar dissolves.

In a large mixing bowl, dissolve yeast in ¼ cup warm water; let stand 5 minutes. Stir in sour cream mixture and egg. Gradually add flour ½ cup at a time to yeast mixture, mixing well. (Dough will be wet.) Cover and chill 8 hours.

Lightly grease muffin pan. Punch dough down. Knead dough lightly 5 or 6 times. Shape into 36 (1-inch) balls; place 3 balls in each muffin cup. Brush with melted butter.

Cover and let rise in a warm place (80 to 85 degrees), 45 minutes or until doubled in size.

Preheat oven to 375 degrees. Bake 10 to 12 minutes or until golden brown. Brush again with melted butter. Freeze up to 1 month, if desired. To reheat, preheat oven to 400 degrees. Wrap frozen rolls in aluminum foil and bake 15 minutes or until thoroughly heated.
Yield: about 1 dozen rolls

Appliquéd Bread Cloth

You will need a 24" square of fabric, matching thread, paper-backed fusible web, green and brown fabric scraps for tree appliqué, black embroidery floss, five red buttons, yellow star button, colander with handles (we used a 5" deep x 14" dia. metal colander), and 2 yds. of 1½"w ribbon.

1. For bread cloth, use matching thread and stitch 1" from edges of fabric square; fray edges.

2. Trace tree and trunk patterns, page 115, onto paper side of fusible web; cut out. Fuse patterns to wrong sides of fabrics; cut out and remove paper backing.
3. Fuse trunk, then tree to one corner of bread cloth. Using three strands of floss, work *Blanket Stitches*, page 154, along edges of tree. Sew buttons to tree.
4. Lay bread cloth right side down in colander; place rolls in bread cloth and fold corners up over rolls.
5. Centering ribbon over top of colander, thread ends of ribbon through handles and bring back to center; tie into a bow.

Tasty Treats to Share
Patterns

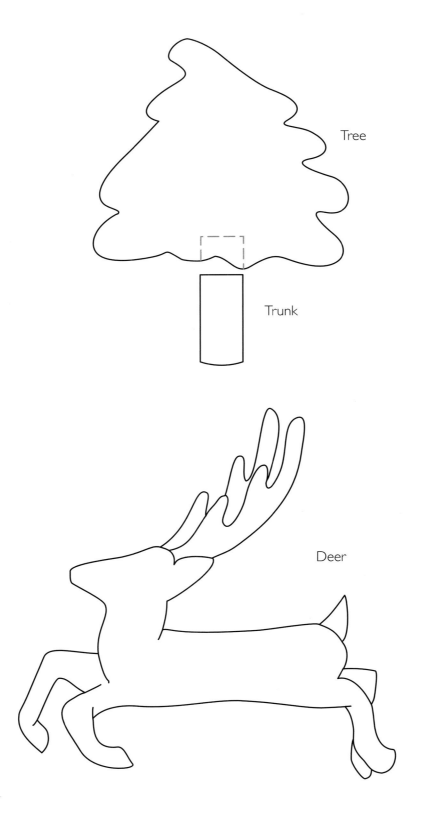

Tree

Trunk

Deer

Nutcracker

Angel

House

Easy Elegance

TUSSIE-MUSSIES
(Shown on page 10)

You will need kraft paper, string, pencil, thumbtack, heavy-duty paper-backed fusible web, gold fabric, white poster board, hot glue gun, lace trim, chenille gimp trim, wide sheer ribbon, and fresh greenery.

To fit our chairs, we made 12"-long tussie-mussies. Adjust sizes and measurements as needed to fit your chairs.

1. To make pattern, cut a 13" square of kraft paper. Tie string to pencil; insert thumbtack 12" from pencil. Refer to Fig. 1 to mark paper. Cut along the drawn line to create a quarter-circle pattern.

Fig. 1

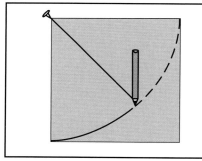

2. Follow manufacturer's instructions to fuse a 13" square of web to wrong side of fabric. Draw around pattern on paper side of fused fabric. Cut out quarter circle, remove paper backing, and fuse fabric to poster board; cut out.
3. Bend sides of quarter circle around each other until point is completely formed. Overlap then, glue edges together at seam.

4. Glue lace trim along top of cone and chenille trim along top edge of lace.
5. Cut one 48" and two 60" lengths of ribbon. Glue center of 48" length two inches from bottom of cone and center of one 60" length at top back of cone.
6. Use ribbons to tie tussie-mussie to chairback. Make a bow using remaining 60" length of ribbon and attach to chair with streamers from top ribbon.
7. Fill the cone with fresh greenery tucked into a sturdy plastic bag to protect inside of tussie-mussie.

GOLD-EMBOSSED PLACE CARDS
(Shown on page 10)

You will need white pre-folded place cards, kraft paper or newsprint, poinsettia-motif rubber stamp to fit on cards, embossing ink stamp pad, metallic gold embossing powder, small paintbrush, embossing pen, embossing heat tool, and a craft knife and cutting mat.

When working with embossing supplies, work on a paper-covered surface. Work quickly, while ink is still wet, to cover surface with embossing powder so it will adhere. After shaking off excess embossing powder, carefully pour the excess back into container for reuse. Follow heat tool manufacturer's instructions to emboss designs.

1. For each place card, open one card flat and lay face up on kraft paper, with fold line horizontal to you.

2. With top of stamp design at least one-third above fold line, stamp flower at center of open card and cover with embossing powder; carefully shake off excess powder, then use paintbrush to lightly brush away any loose powder flecks.
3. Use embossing pen to write name on card and cover with embossing powder; carefully shake off excess powder, then use paintbrush to lightly brush away any loose powder flecks.
4. Use heat tool to emboss designs.
5. To make stamped design stand up when card is folded, use craft knife to carefully cut around design above fold line.

RIBBON NAPKIN RINGS
(Shown on page 10)

You will need paper towel tubes, 1 1/2"w ribbon, fabric glue, 1/16" dia. metallic gold cord, liquid fray preventative, and greenery sprigs.

Allow glue to dry after each application; hold embellishments in place with straight pins until dry.

1. For each napkin ring, cut a 1 1/4"w ring from tube.
2. Measure around ring; add 1/2". Cut two lengths of ribbon the determined measurement. Overlapping ends, glue one ribbon length around inside and one around outside of ring.
3. Cut lengths of cord to fit along top and bottom edges of ring; apply fray preventative to ends of cord lengths and allow to dry. Glue cord lengths in place on ring.
4. With ribbon overlap at top and a piece of greenery covering overlap, wrap a length of cord around ring several times, then tie into a bow; trim cord ends, apply fray preventative, and allow to dry.

PARTY FAVORS
(Shown on page 12)

You will need tracing paper, sturdy Christmas-motif wrapping paper, $1/4$" dia. hole punch, self-adhesive hole reinforcement labels (clear or a color that won't show through wrapping paper), craft glue stick, $1/4$"w gold ribbon, and gifts or goodies to fit inside favors.

1. Trace pattern, page 120, onto tracing paper; cut out. For each favor, draw around pattern on wrong side of wrapping paper; cut out.
2. Punch four holes in paper as indicated on pattern; attach reinforcements around holes on wrong side of paper.
3. Fold each long side edge $1/4$" to wrong side as indicated on pattern; fold paper in half. Glue right sides of folded side edges together to form cup and allow to dry.
4. Refer to Diagram 1 to thread ribbon through holes and create handle. Place gift in cup.
5. Refer to Diagram 2 to use handle as one loop in each bow and to tie a bow on each side of favor; notch ribbon ends.

You can decide on the perfect party favor to tuck away in these merry little containers, but here are a few ideas to get you thinking:

- Chocolates, mints, or nuts
- Sachets or potpourri
- Charms
- Tiny ornaments
- Holiday refrigerator magnets
- Stickers
- Rubber stamps
- Miniature figurines
- "Coupons" for complementary babysitting - maybe while your guests are holiday shopping.

DIAGRAM 1

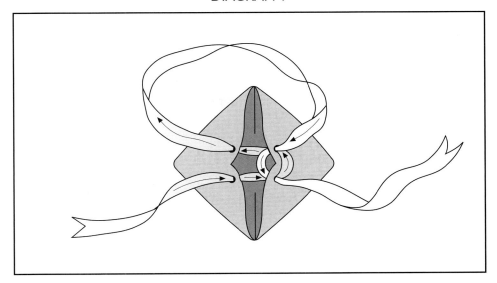

DIAGRAM 2

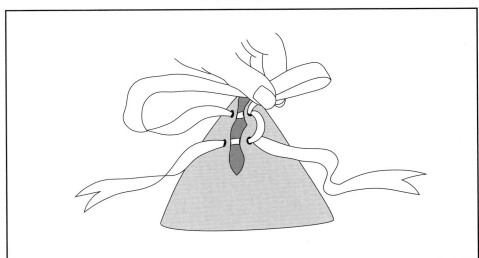

PARTY FAVOR

BEADED ORNAMENTS
(Shown on page 15)

For each Beaded Ornament, cover a shiny glass ball ornament with an arrangement of strips and punched shapes of double-sided adhesive mounting paper (we used photo scrapbooking supplies). Then peel away the paper and press tiny glass marbles into the exposed adhesive. Finish with a bow of metallic cord tied around the ornament cap; secure with glue if necessary.

Use a wet fingertip or the sticky side of a self-adhesive note to pick up and apply the beads.

BUFFET ARRANGEMENT
(Shown on page 16)

It is easy to create a glistening arrangement to bring the splendor of the holidays to your buffet. Simply place blocks of water-soaked floral foam on a plastic-covered tray and stack candle-filled goblets on top. Cover foam with sprigs of fresh greenery for a fragrant and festive effect. Add a big ribbon bow and surround the arrangement with a length of lush artificial garland. Accent with gold and red berry sprays and magnolia leaves dry-brushed with gold and silver paint. Gold glass ball ornaments lend opulence to the magnificent display.

The ideal height for a centerpiece is at a level that won't block the line of sight between guests. A quick and easy way to check maximum height as you construct your centerpiece is to rest your elbow on the table and bend your arm upward at a ninety-degree angle, then make a fist. If the height of your centerpiece exceeds the height of your hand, adjust your centerpiece accordingly.

PARTY FAVOR PATTERN

Candle Light, Burning Bright

HURRICANE CANDLEHOLDER

(Shown on page 22)

You will need a 3" dia. x 9"h pillar candle; utility scissors; medium-weight craft steel; scrap of craft foam; two 1"-long brass brads with large heads; gold seed beads; 6mm gold jewelry washers; $\frac{1}{2}$"-long gold sequin pins; wire cutters; 20-gauge craft wire in gold, silver, and copper; three strands of various-sized gold and silver beaded garland; and a 12"h glass hurricane candleholder.

1. For steel cuff, measure circumference of candle and add 1"; cut a strip of steel 3"w by the determined measurement. Referring to cuff diagram, place strip on foam and use a stylus to draw swirls along center of strip. Use a hammer and small nail to punch a hole in strip at center of each swirl; punch rows of equally spaced holes $\frac{1}{4}$" from top and bottom edges of cuff.

2. Wrap cuff around candle, aligning holes and overlapping ends at center back. Push one brad into candle through each center back hole at top and bottom edge of cuff to secure. For decorative studs, slip one seed bead, then one washer onto a sequin pin. Pushing into candle, insert one stud into every fourth hole along edges and into each center hole in swirls.

3. For wire tie, cut one yard each of gold, silver, and copper wire. Leaving a 2" tail on each end, twist the three wires together. Beginning and ending at center front, wrap twisted wire around cuff three times. Twist ends together to make a "bow," then wrap each wire end around a pencil to curl ends.

4. Coil one strand of beaded garland in bottom of candleholder, then center candle on top of coil. Check for stability, then carefully wind remaining garlands around candle.

SPIRAL BEADED TAPERS

(Shown on page 22)

For each taper, you will need craft glue, one $2\frac{1}{2}$" and one 3" or 4" dia. decorative wooden circle cutout, metallic gold and white acrylic paint, paintbrushes, one $2\frac{1}{2}$" wooden snowflake cutout, opalescent glitter, drill and long thin countersink bit, long thin screw (depth of base plus 1"), 8"h dripless taper candle, wire cutters, 20-gauge gold craft wire, and assorted clear frosted and crystal beads.

Note: As candle burns, adjust height of spiral by pushing wire down towards base of candle.

Allow glue and paint to dry after each application.

1. For candle base, center and glue smaller wooden circle to center of larger wooden circle. Paint base gold and snowflake white. Apply a thin coat of glue over top and edges of snowflake; sprinkle with glitter, then shake off excess. Center and glue snowflake to top of base.

2. Working from the bottom, mark center and countersink a pilot hole through all layers of base. Insert screw with tip protruding 1" through top. Center candle over screw and gently twist until bottom of candle is flush with base.

3. For beaded spiral, cut a 36" length of wire. Insert one end of wire into base of candle; thread with desired beads as you spiral wire upwards around candle. Bend remaining wire end to secure beads.

BEADED DOILY

(Shown on page 22)

Make a special "tablecloth" for a pedestal cake stand with a scallop-edged doily decorated with beaded dangles. Using a needle and sewing thread, take a small securing stitch at the center of one lace scallop, then thread crystal beads as follows: one 4mm round, two 2mm seed, one 9mm bugle, two 2mm seed, one large drop crystal, and end with one 2mm seed. Bring the thread around the outside of the last seed bead, back up through the center of all beads and knot off at the beginning point on scallop. Repeat for remaining scallops. Place doily on stand.

CANDLE CUFF

CUFF DIAGRAM

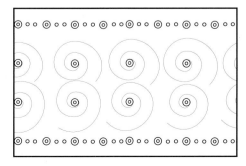

Lakeside Cabin Christmas

CANDLE-LIT LANTERNS
(Shown on page 24)

For each lantern, you will need a 12" square of 36-gauge brass tooling foil, utility scissors, newspaper, tape, awl, hammer, two brass paper fasteners, flat screwdriver with a $1/4$"w tip, $1/4$" dia. brass grommet kit, two 36" lengths of 16-gauge galvanized wire, half-gallon glass jar, pliers, sand, and a pillar candle.

1. For shade, enlarge pattern, page 129, 146%; cut out. Draw around pattern on foil; cut out.
2. Place shade, right side up, on a thick layer of newspaper for padding. Tape pattern to foil. Punching through pattern and foil, use awl and hammer to make inner and outer circles of holes and to make holes for paper fasteners along back overlap. Make holes where indicated for wire handle; use screwdriver to enlarge holes to fit grommets. Turn shade over and use screwdriver to make decorative indentions along inner and outer edges of shade. Follow manufacturer's instructions to install grommets.
3. With right side up, overlap shade until fastener holes line up. Working from outside, insert fasteners in holes and open prongs flat on inside.
4. For handle, refer to Fig. 1 and wrap one length of wire around neck of jar below threads; twist wire around itself to secure. Repeat on opposite side of jar with remaining wire. Use pliers to shape a single loop in each wire, $1^1/2$" above rim of jar.

Fig. 1

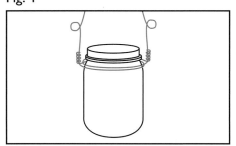

5. Thread ends of wire through grommets in shade; slide shade onto wires until shade rests on loops in wire. Use pliers to twist handle wires together several times about 8" above shade. Wrap wire ends around a pencil to shape tendrils.
6. Slide shade to top of handle. Pour sand into jar; center candle in sand. Replace shade.

NATURAL GARLAND
(Shown on page 27)

You will need a drill and small bit, assorted dried natural pods and nutshells, wire cutters, 22-gauge rusted craft wire, and a pencil.

1. Carefully drill holes through centers of pods and nutshells.
2. Double the desired finished length of garland and cut a length of wire this measurement.
3. Leaving a 6" length of wire free at one end, wrap wire two to three times around pencil to curl; remove pencil. Thread on one natural, wrap wire around pencil again and thread on another natural; repeat process until 6" of wire remains at other end.
4. For hanger, make a loop in wire at each end of garland and twist wire around itself to secure.

GOURD BIRDHOUSE
(Shown on page 27)

You will need a craft knife, large cured gourd, small stick for perch, hot glue gun, 26-gauge rusted craft wire, wire cutters, short pieces of greenery, and artificial berry vine.

1. Using tip of craft knife, make a pilot hole in gourd; "drill" and then scrape edges of hole to $1^1/2$" diameter. Repeat to make a smaller hole to fit stick for perch; make one small hole on each side of gourd near top to thread hanger through.
2. Insert stick into perch hole and glue to secure. Thread an 18" length of wire through hanger holes and twist ends together to secure.
3. Twisting wire around each greenery stem to secure, make a garland to fit around top of birdhouse; wrap berry vine around garland, securing with lengths of wire.

FLEECE STOCKINGS
(Shown on page 30)

For each stocking, you will need red polyester fleece, black embroidery floss, paper-backed fusible web, pressing cloth, black felt, $4^1/2$" x $8^1/2$" piece of chamois, and pinking shears.

Refer to Embroidery Stitches, page 154, before beginning project. Use six strands of floss for all embroidery.

1. For pattern, enlarge stocking pattern, page 128, 160%; cut out. Use pattern to cut stocking front and back from fleece.
2. Matching edges, place stocking pieces together. Leaving top edge unstitched, use floss and work *Blanket Stitches* along edges of stocking.
3. For cuff, trace bear pattern, page 126, onto paper side of web; do not remove paper backing. Using pressing cloth, fuse bear to felt; cut out bear along drawn lines and remove paper backing. Fuse bear to center of chamois piece. Trim one long and both short edges of chamois with pinking shears. Matching straight edge of cuff to top front edge of stocking, use floss and work *Straight Stitches* to attach cuff to stocking.
4. For hanger, cut a $1/2$" x 7" strip of felt; tack ends to inside of stocking at heel side seam.

CHAMOIS ORNAMENTS

(Shown on page 32)

For each ornament, you will need one 9¹/₂"w x 8³/₄"-long piece and one ¹/₄"w x 3"-long strip of leather chamois, fabric glue, 3" dia. plastic foam ball, two rubber bands, 20" length of leather lacing, two 10mm black wooden beads, and a 10" length of heavy monofilament.

1. For fringe, draw a line 2" from one short edge of chamois piece; make cuts from edge to drawn line at ¹/₄" intervals.
2. Apply a line of glue along one long edge of chamois. Center ball on chamois; wrap chamois around ball, overlapping edges at center back; allow to dry.
3. Use rubber bands to gather chamois close to ball at top and bottom. For top of ornament, leaving 3" streamers, wrap lacing around rubber band; tie streamers into a knot at center front. Slip one bead onto each streamer, then knot end of lacing. For bottom of ornament, glue chamois strip over rubber band.
4. For hanger, thread monofilament through top of ornament; knot ends together to form a loop.

FLEECE TREE SKIRT

(Shown on page 32)

You will need 1²/₃ yds. red polyester fleece, string, removable fabric marking pen, thumbtack, black embroidery floss, tracing paper, pinking shears, chamois, paper-backed fusible web, pressing cloth, black felt, and fabric glue.

1. Fold fleece in half from top to bottom and again from left to right. Tie one end of string to pen. Insert thumbtack through string 30" from pen for outer cutting line. Insert thumbtack through folded corner of fabric as shown in Fig. 1; draw outer cutting line.

Fig. 1

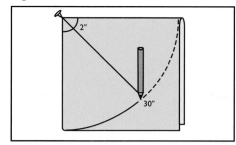

2. Reinsert thumbtack through string 2" from pen and draw inner cutting line. Cut along drawn lines through all fabric layers. For opening in back of skirt, cut through one layer of fabric along one fold line from outer to inner edge.
3. Unfold skirt, then draw a stitching line 3" above bottom edge. For fringe, make cuts from bottom edge of skirt to stitching line at ¹/₂" intervals. Using six strands of floss and clips in fabric to position stitches evenly, work *Blanket Stitches*, page 154, along stitching line.
4. For appliqués, trace oval pattern, page 127, onto tracing paper; cut out. Use pattern and pinking shears to cut nine ovals from chamois. Leaving 1" between shapes, trace nine bear patterns, page 126, onto paper side of web; do not remove paper backing. Cut out each bear ¹/₂" outside drawn line. Using pressing cloth, fuse bears to felt; cut out bears along drawn lines, remove paper backing, and fuse one bear to center of each oval.
5. Spacing evenly, glue appliqués along bottom of skirt, 6" from top of fringe; allow to dry.

DECORATIVE BIRDHOUSES

(Shown on page 34)

You will need assorted wooden birdhouses; tall wooden turnings or candlesticks, ball knobs, circles, or squares to embellish houses; paintbrushes; white acrylic paint; sandpaper; tack cloth; wood glue; wood screws; utility scissors; scraps of metal flashing and metal ceiling tiles; ¹/₂"-long brads; pliers, and items for perches (we used a key, drawer pull, and a bolt).

Allow paint and glue to dry after each application.

After we built our birdhouses, we set them outside for several weeks to let them "weather."

1. Paint birdhouses and wooden pieces white; allow to dry. Lightly sand for a weathered look; wipe with tack cloth. Use wood glue and screws to attach wooden pieces to birdhouses as desired.
2. For scalloped roof, measure thickness of roof and add ¹/₄"; measure length of one side of slope of roof. Use utility scissors to cut two strips of flashing the determined measurements. Draw scallops along one long edge of each strip; cut out. Overlapping at peak of roof, use brads to attach strips to roof. Measure up one side of roof to peak and down opposite side; measure roof from front to back. Cut a piece of flashing the determined measurements. Bend flashing roof in half, place on birdhouse, and use brads to attach.
3. For front-overlapped roof, measure up one side of roof to peak and down opposite side; measure roof from front to back plus the thickness of roof then add ¹/₂". Cut a piece of ceiling tile the determined measurements. Bend tile roof in half, then matching back edges, place on birdhouse and use brads to attach. Bending and overlapping at front peak, use plies to bend tile roof over front of birdhouse roof; use brads to attach.
4. For plain roof, measure up one side of roof to peak and down opposite side; measure roof from front to back. Cut a piece of ceiling tile the determined measurements. Bend tile roof in half, then matching edges, place on birdhouse and use brads to attach.
5. Attach item for perch to front of birdhouse.

HOLLY LEAF PILLOW
(Shown on page 34)

You will need tissue paper, two 15" squares of chenille fabric, skein of green crewel yarn, three red buttons (we used one $7/8$" dia. and two $3/4$" dia. buttons), 14" square pillow form, and $1^3/4$ yds. of ball fringe.

Refer to Embroidery Stitches, page 154, before beginning project. Use a $1/2$" seam allowance for all sewing.

1. Enlarge holly leaves pattern, page 125, 140%, then trace onto tissue paper. Center and pin tissue paper pattern to right side of one pillow square.
2. Using one strand of yarn, and stitching through the pattern, *Backstitch* holly leaves on pillow front; carefully tear away pattern. Sew buttons in a cluster at center of design.
3. Matching right sides and leaving bottom edge open for turning and inserting pillow form, sew pillow squares together. Clip corners, then turn right side out. Insert pillow form; sew opening closed.
4. Beginning and ending at center bottom, whipstitch fringe around pillow along seamline.

RAG PILLOW
(Shown on page 35)

For each pillow, you will need a fabric marking pen, rag rug for pillow front, 2 yds. of $1^1/2$"w brush fringe, 17" square of chenille fabric for pillow back, and a 16" square pillow form.

Use a $1/2$" seam allowance for all sewing.

1. Use marking pen and a ruler to draw a 17" square on rug. To prevent rug from unraveling, stitch around square just inside drawn line; cut out on drawn line.

2. Matching flange of fringe to raw edges of fabric, pin, then baste trim along edges on right side of chenille square.
3. Matching right sides and leaving bottom edge open for turning and inserting pillow form, sew pillow pieces together. Clip corners, then turn right side out. Insert pillow form; sew opening closed.

ENVELOPE PILLOW
(Shown on page 35)

You will need a 7" x 17" piece of an old quilt for flap, 1" dia. and $1/2$" dia. buttons, two 13" x 17" pieces of chenille fabric for pillow front and back, polyester fiberfill, and $2/3$ yd. of $1^1/4$"w vintage crocheted trim.

Use a $1/2$" seam allowance for all sewing.

1. For flap, refer to Fig. 1 to cut a triangle from quilt piece. Baste around triangle $1/2$" from raw edges. Press short raw edges of flap to right side along stitching line.

Fig. 1

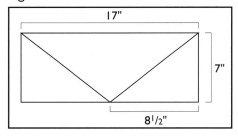

2. Use a zigzag stitch to sew trim over pressed raw edges of flap. Stack, then sew buttons to point of flap.
3. With right sides up and matching raw edges, lay flap on top of one pillow front; baste raw edges together.
4. Matching right sides and leaving bottom edge open for turning and stuffing, sew pillow front and back together. Clip corners, turn right side out, and stuff with fiberfill; sew opening closed.

CEILING TILE POCKET
(Shown on page 35)

You will need a hammer, awl, 12"w x 24"-long piece of tin ceiling tile, two 60" lengths of 16-gauge galvanized wire, pliers, and assorted greenery.

1. Referring to Fig. 1, use hammer and awl to punch evenly spaced holes along each side of tile. Matching holes, bend tile in half.

Fig. 1

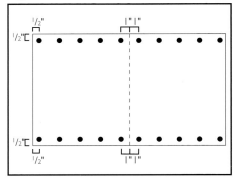

2. Working with one length of wire for each side and beginning at bottom fold, lace sides together. Twist excess wire from each side together at top to form handle.
3. Fill pocket with assorted greenery.

To keep live greenery fresh and lasting through the holidays, place a piece of water-soaked floral foam (cut to fit in your container) in a heavy-duty plastic freezer storage bag. Slip the bag into your Ceiling Tile Pocket, then arrange assorted greenery, inserting the stems into the foam.

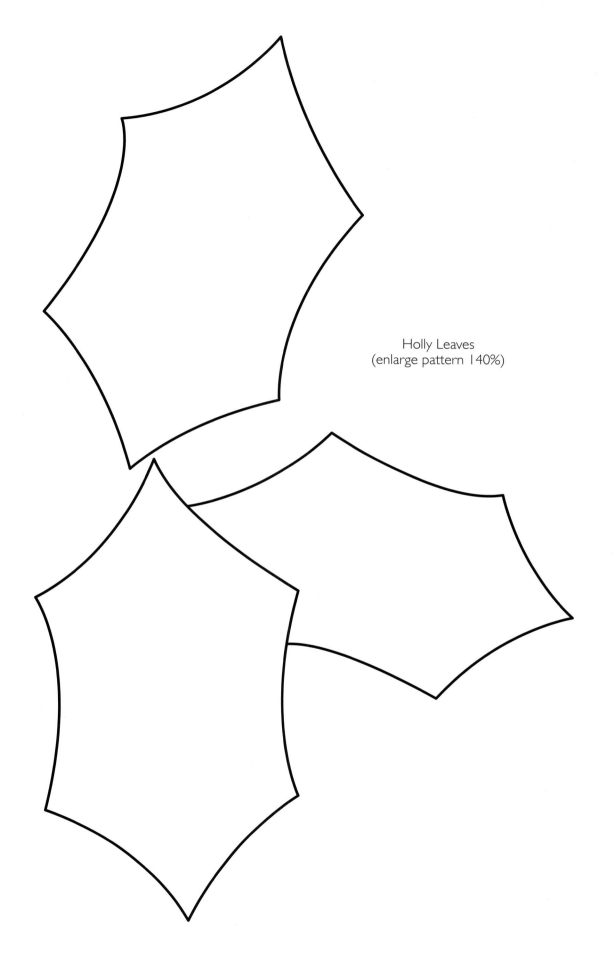

Holly Leaves
(enlarge pattern 140%)

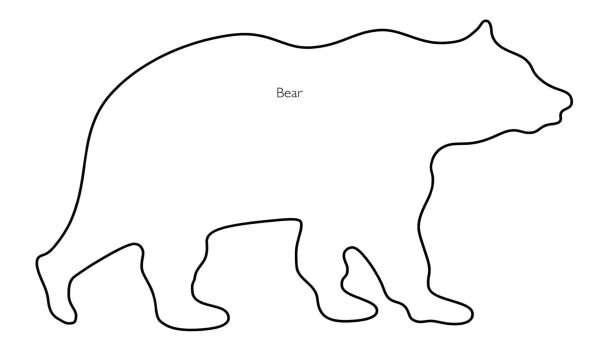

Bear

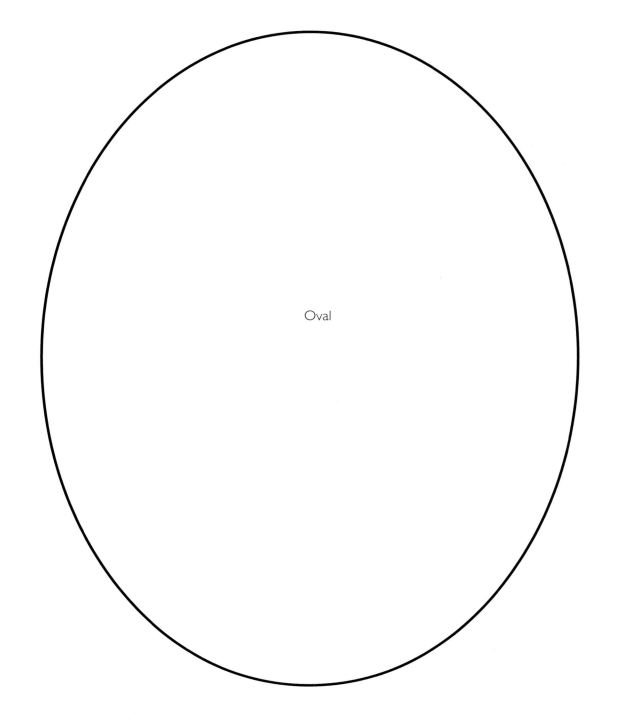

Oval

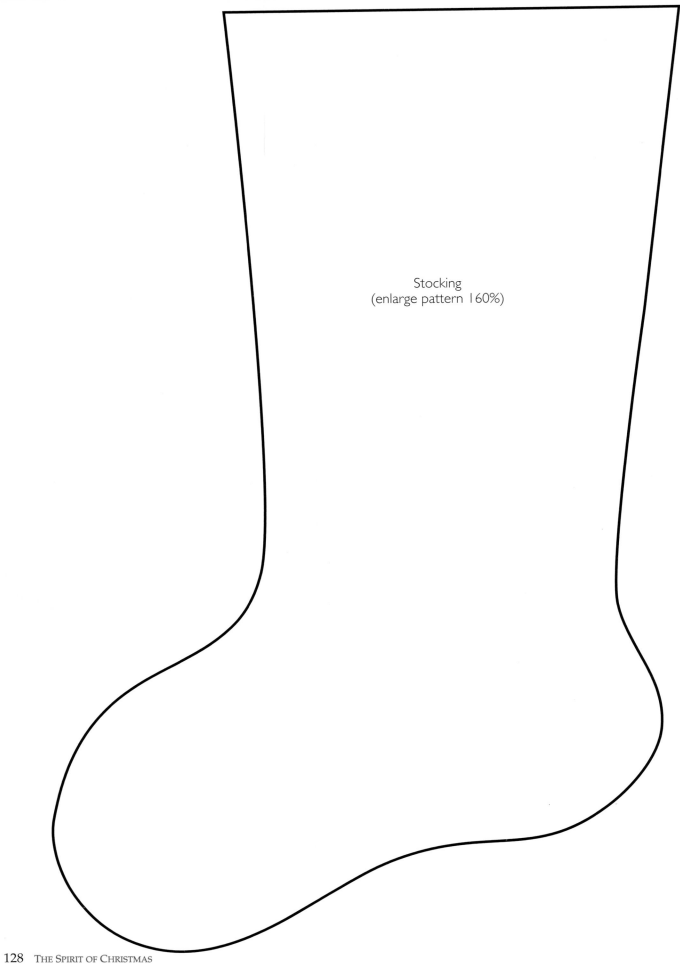

Stocking
(enlarge pattern 160%)

Shade
(enlarge pattern 146%)

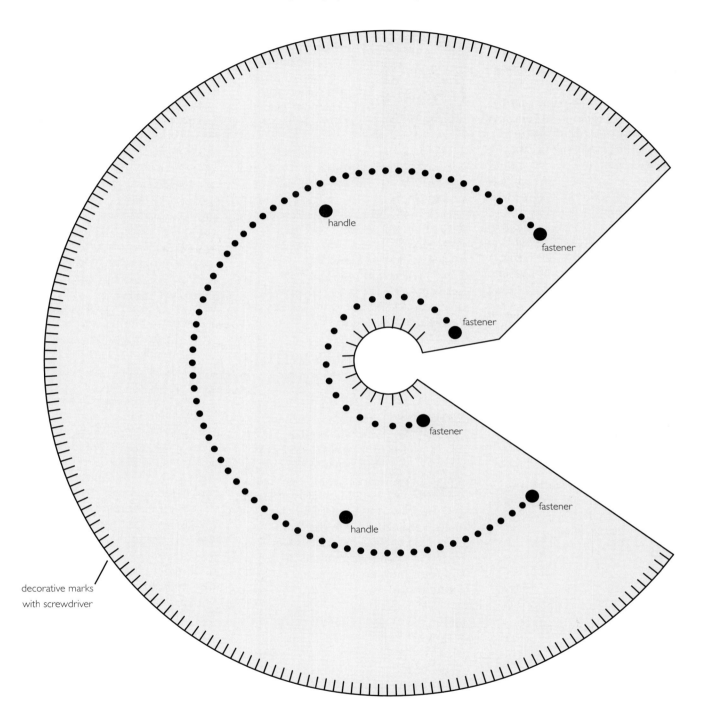

handle

fastener

fastener

fastener

fastener

handle

decorative marks
with screwdriver

Winter Majesty

FAUX MARBLE PEDESTAL

(Shown on page 41)

You will need white primer, plaster pedestal (ours measures 14"h); paintbrushes; white, blue, and grey-blue acrylic paint; glazing medium; large feather or liner paintbrush; sponge; and high gloss acrylic spray sealer.

1. Apply two coats of primer, then white paint to pedestal and allow to dry.
2. Using white, blue, and grey-blue paints, mix three separate glazes. Make each glaze by mixing two parts clear glazing medium with one part paint.
3. For veining, working in small sections, apply a coat of white glaze. While glaze is still wet, use liner brush or feather to make a jagged diagonal line of blue glaze. Lightly blend edges of line with damp sponge to achieve a shadowy, uneven look. Repeat process until entire pedestal is covered.
4. Drag liner brush or feather dipped in grey-blue glaze across blended areas to accent vein. Allow to dry.
5. Using a clean damp feather, apply a coat of white glaze in a jagged back and forth motion over painted surface to create a milky appearance. Allow to dry. Finish with a coat of high gloss sealer.

BEADED SNOWFLAKE BALL ORNAMENTS

(Shown on page 42)

For each ornament, you will need craft glue, micro paint tip (to fit on glue bottle), 2¹/₂" dia. silver glass ball ornament, and crystal micro beads.

1. Using glue with paint tip attached and working on one section at a time, paint a snowflake on ornament. Pour beads over wet glue, covering design completely; tap ornament lightly to remove excess beads. Spacing as desired, work around ornament adding additional snowflakes.
2. When dry, apply dots of glue between snowflakes and cover with beads; tap ornament lightly to remove excess beads. Hang to dry.

FROSTED BALLS WITH BEADED COLLARS

(Shown on page 41)

For each ornament, you will need a 3¹/₄" dia. frosted glass ball ornament, beading thread, beading needle, liquid fray preventative, and the following beads: 384 clear and silver-lined seed, eight 5mm crystal bicone, 252 sterling silver seed, eight 5mm crystal teardrop, and four 5mm opalescent round beads.

Note: Because sterling silver will tarnish, store loose beads and beaded ornaments in resealable plastic bags out of season.

Refer to Beading Basics, page 136, and Collar Beading Diagrams, page 131, to complete each row of collar. Thread needle with a 1¹/₂ yd. length of thread to begin, adding new thread as needed.

1. For Row 1, leaving a 3" tail and locking first bead in place, thread one bicone bead and ten assorted seed beads. Repeat beading pattern three more times. Thread needle through locking bead twice to secure Row 1; place on ornament.
2. For Row 2, thread 25 sterling seed beads, then thread needle through the next bicone bead in Row 1 to complete scallop. Repeat beading pattern three more times.
3. For Row 3, thread eighteen assorted seed beads, one teardrop bead, and eighteen assorted seed beads, then thread needle through the next bicone bead in Row 1 to complete scallop. Repeat beading pattern three more times. Thread needle through the next eighteen assorted seed beads and teardrop bead in Row 3.
4. For Row 4, thread fourteen sterling seed beads, one bicone bead, and fourteen sterling seed beads, then thread needle through the next teardrop bead in Row 3. Repeat beading pattern three more times.
5. For Row 5, thread 25 assorted seed beads, then thread needle through next bicone bead in Row 4. Thread ten sterling seed beads, one round bead, and one teardrop bead; double back through round bead, sterling seed beads, and bicone bead. Thread 25 assorted seed beads, then thread needle through next teardrop bead in Row 3. Repeat beading pattern three more times.
6. Thread needle through first seed bead in Row 5 twice to lock in place. Secure thread ends to complete collar.

COLLAR BEADING DIAGRAMS

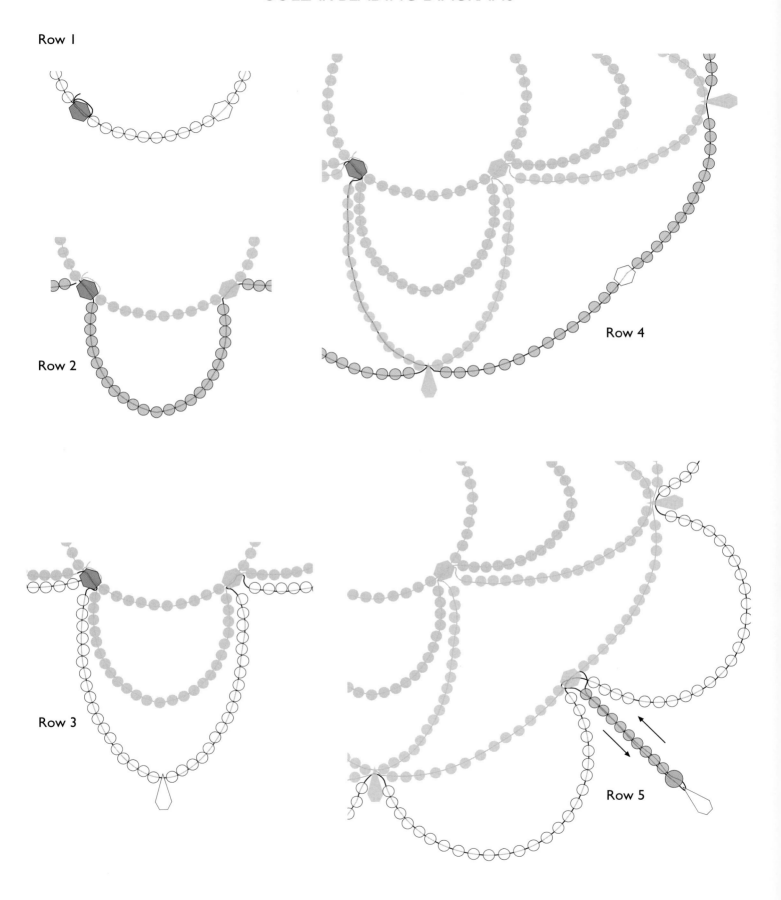

Row 1

Row 2

Row 3

Row 4

Row 5

FROSTED SNOWFLAKE BALL ORNAMENTS
(Shown on pages 39 and 41)

For each ornament, you will need one 2¼" dia. opalescent glass ornament and one 2½" dia. clear glass ornament, rubbing alcohol, various sizes of self-adhesive snowflake stickers, pencils or dowel pieces and a block of plastic foam, white frosted glass spray finish, craft knife, and a 12" length of sheer wire-edged ribbon.

To hold ornaments while applying finish and drying, remove metal end caps and place ornaments on the eraser end of a pencil or dowel piece inserted into a block of plastic foam.

1. Wipe ornaments with alcohol and allow to dry. Adhere stickers to ornament as desired.
2. Remove metal end caps. Following manufacturer's instructions, spray ornaments with finish and allow to dry. Use craft knife to carefully remove stickers; carefully replace end caps.
3. Tie one ornament to each end of ribbon, trim ends. To hang, drape ribbon over tree branch.

BEADED SWIRL BALL ORNAMENTS
(Shown on page 41)

For each ornament, you will need craft glue, micro paint tip (to fit on glue bottle), 2½" dia. white frosted glass ornament, and silver micro beads.

1. Using glue with paint tip attached and working on one section at a time, paint a swirl on ornament. Pour beads over wet glue, covering design completely; tap ornament lightly to remove excess beads and allow to dry. Spacing as desired, work around ornament adding additional swirls.
2. When dry, apply dots of glue between swirls and cover with beads; tap ornament lightly to remove excess beads. Hang to dry.

TUCKED CUFF STOCKING
(Shown on page 42)

You will need two 12" x 20" pieces of fabric for stocking front and back, two 12" x 20" pieces of fabric for stocking overlay (we used a sheer embossed fabric), two 12" x 20" pieces of fabric for stocking lining (we used opalescent voile), 8" x 15½" piece of fabric for cuff (we used silver pre-tucked silk), beading needle, 4mm glass beads, silver seed beads, and a 9" length of ½"w ribbon.

Use ½" seam allowance for all sewing.

1. For pattern, enlarge stocking pattern, page 137, 160%; cut out.
2. Place right sides of stocking fabric pieces together and use pattern to cut out stocking. Place right sides of overlay fabric together and use pattern to cut out stocking overlay. With right sides facing up, baste overlay front to stocking front. Repeat for stocking back. Matching right sides of fabric and leaving top edges open, sew stocking front and back together. Clip curves and turn right side out.
3. For lining, place right sides of lining fabric pieces together; use pattern to cut out stocking lining. Matching right sides of fabric and leaving top edges open, sew stocking lining front and back together. Clip curves; do not turn right side out. With wrong sides together and matching side seams, insert lining into stocking. Baste lining to stocking along top edges.
4. For hanger, fold ribbon in half and, with raw edges of ribbon extending ½" beyond raw edge of stocking top, baste hanger inside stocking to heel side seam.
5. For cuff, use beading needle to sew one glass bead topped with one seed bead at each intersection of fabric tucks. Matching right sides and short edges of cuff, sew short edges together; press seam open. Matching wrong sides and long edges, fold cuff in half. Matching raw edges, insert cuff into top of stocking; sew cuff to stocking along raw edges. Turn cuff to outside.

TUCKED AND BEADED STOCKING
(Shown on page 42)

You will need two 12" x 20" pieces of pre-tucked silk fabric for stocking front and back (we used silver), two 12" x 20" pieces of fabric for stocking lining (we used opalescent voile), 8" x 15½" piece of fabric for cuff (we used opalescent voile), beading needle, 4mm glass beads, silver seed beads, 9" length of ½"w ribbon, and a 15" length of beaded trim with flange.

Use ½" seam allowance for all sewing.

1. For pattern, enlarge stocking pattern, page 137, 160%; cut out.
2. Place right sides of stocking fabric pieces together and use pattern to cut out stocking. For stocking front, on right side of fabric, use beading needle to sew one glass bead topped with one seed bead at each intersection of fabric tucks. Leaving top edges open, sew stocking pieces together. Clip curves and turn right side out.
3. For lining, place right sides of lining fabric pieces together; use pattern to cut out stocking lining. Matching right sides of fabric and leaving top edges open, sew stocking lining front and back together. Clip curves; do not turn right side out. With wrong sides together and matching side seams, insert lining into stocking. Baste lining to stocking along top edges.
4. For hanger, fold ribbon in half and, with raw edges of ribbon extending ½" beyond raw edge of stocking top, baste hanger inside stocking to heel side seam.
5. For cuff, matching right sides and short edges of cuff fabric piece, sew short edges together; press seam open. Matching wrong sides and long edges, fold cuff in half. Matching raw edges and right sides, insert cuff into top of stocking; sew cuff to stocking along raw edges. Turn cuff to outside.
6. Beginning and ending at side seam, whipstitch beaded trim along bottom edge of cuff.

CRYSTAL SNOWFLAKE ORNAMENTS

(Shown on page 42)

Refer to photo on page 42; Snowflake instructions are in clockwise order beginning from top left of photo.

Note: Because sterling silver will tarnish, store loose beads and beaded ornaments in resealable plastic bags out of season.

Refer to Beading Basics, page 136, before making projects.

SNOWFLAKE ORNAMENT A

For each snowflake, you will need 32-gauge beading wire, wire cutters, needle nose pliers, and the following beads: thirteen 8mm crystal faceted, twenty-four 15mm iridescent bugle, twelve 4mm white faceted, and twelve 4mm sterling silver round.

1. For center circle, work counter-clockwise. Leaving a 3" tail, refer to Fig. A1 and thread six 8mm faceted beads on a 1½ yd length of wire. Thread wire through first bead to form a circle. Twist tail tightly around wire close to first bead; trim tail. Thread one faceted bead to center of circle; thread wire from right to left through bead on opposite side of circle.

Fig. A1

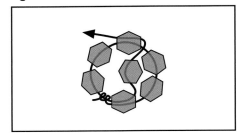

2. For snowflake points, refer to Fig. A2 and thread one bugle, one 4mm round, one bugle, one 4mm faceted, one 8mm faceted, and one 4mm faceted bead onto wire; double back through faceted beads, using pliers to bend wire close to last bead at point. Thread one bugle, one 4mm round, and one bugle bead onto wire; thread wire from right to left through 8mm faceted bead on circle again. Thread wire through next bead on center circle. Repeat beading pattern five more times. Thread wire through two 8mm faceted beads on center circle; twist around center circle wire.

Fig. A2

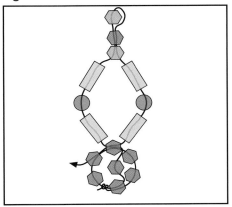

3. For hanger, fold remaining wire into a loop. Twist wire end around center circle wire at base of loop; trim excess.

SNOWFLAKE ORNAMENT B

For each snowflake, you will need 24-gauge beading wire, wire cutters, needle nose pliers, and the following beads: six 5mm crystal faceted, eighteen 4mm transparent bicone, twelve 25mm silver bugle, seven large assorted crystal, 24 clear silver-lined seed, and six 8mm clear heart-shaped.

1. For outer circle, work counter-clockwise. Leaving a 3" tail, refer to Fig. B1 and thread one faceted and two bicone beads on a 1½ yd. length of wire. Repeat beading pattern five more times. Thread wire through first faceted bead to form a circle, then twist tail around wire close to first bead; trim tail.

Fig B1

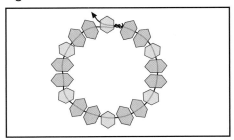

2. For snowflake points, refer to Fig. B2 and thread one bugle, one bicone, one large assorted, and one seed bead onto wire; double back through large assorted and bicone beads, using pliers to bend wire close to seed bead at point. Thread one bugle bead onto wire, then thread wire from right to left through faceted bead on outer circle again. Thread wire through next two bicone beads and faceted bead on outer circle. Repeat beading pattern five more times. Thread wire through next bicone bead on outer circle. Twist around center circle wire.

Fig. B2

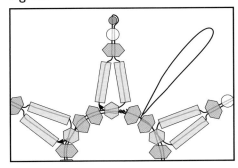

3. For hanger, fold remaining wire into a loop. Twist wire end around outer circle wire at base of loop; trim excess.

4. *(Refer to Beading Diagrams B1 and B2, below, for Steps 4 and 5.)* For snowflake center and first two spokes, tie on a 1 yd. length of wire between two bicone beads on outer circle wire, then thread one seed, one heart-shaped, one seed, one large bead from assortment, and three seed beads; double back and thread wire through large bead. Thread on three more seed beads, then double back through large bead again.

5. Thread one seed, one heart-shaped, and one seed bead onto wire. Wrap wire around outer circle between two bicone beads. Double back through beads on spoke.

6. (*Note:* For remaining spokes, work counterclockwise.) Pick up next seed bead on inner circle, then repeat Step 5 to make two more spokes. Passing under first spoke, pick up next seed bead on inner circle and repeat Step 5 to make remaining two spokes. Double back through last spoke and remaining seed bead on inner circle. Twist wire end tightly around next spoke; trim excess.

BEADING DIAGRAM B1

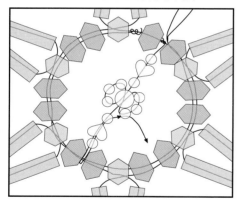

BEADING DIAGRAM B2

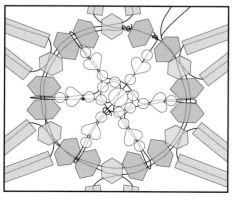

SNOWFLAKE ORNAMENT C

For each snowflake, you will need 32-gauge beading wire, wire cutters, needle nose pliers, and the following beads: six 5mm opalescent round, forty-two 4mm white faceted, thirty-six 7mm crystal twisted bugle, and six 4mm transparent bicone.

1. For center circle, work counterclockwise. Leaving a 3" tail, refer to Fig. C1 and thread one round and one faceted bead on a 1½ yd. length of wire. Repeat beading pattern five more times. Thread wire through first round bead to form a circle, then twist tail tightly around wire close to first bead; trim tail.

Fig. C1

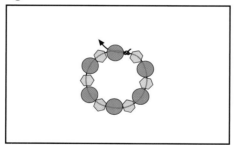

2. For snowflake points, refer to Fig. C2 and thread one bugle, one faceted, one bugle, one faceted, one bugle, one faceted, one bicone, and one faceted bead onto wire; double back through bicone and faceted beads, using pliers to bend wire close to faceted bead at point. Thread one bugle, one faceted, one bugle, one faceted, and one bugle bead onto wire; thread wire from right to left through first round bead on circle again. Thread wire through next faceted and round beads on center circle. Repeat beading pattern five more times. Twist wire around center circle wire.

Fig. C2

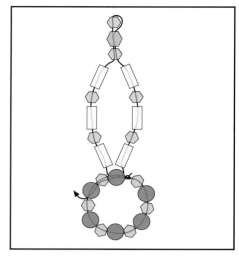

3. For hanger, fold remaining wire into a loop. Twist wire end around center circle wire at base of loop; trim excess.

SNOWFLAKE ORNAMENT D

For each snowflake, you will need 32-gauge beading wire, wire cutters, needle nose pliers, and the following beads: twelve 8mm crystal faceted, six 9mm melon twelve 25mm silver bugle, nineteen silver-lined pebble beads and one 12mm melon bead.

1. For outer circle, work counterclockwise. Leaving a 3" tail, refer to Fig. D1 and thread one 8mm faceted, one bugle, one 8mm faceted, and one pebble bead on a 1½ yd length of wire. Double back through 8mm faceted bead, using pliers to bend wire close to pebble bead. Thread one bugle bead. Thread wire from right to left through first 8mm faceted bead. Thread one pebble bead and thread wire from right to left back through first 8mm faceted bead.

Thread one 9mm melon and one pebble bead. Thread wire back through 9mm melon bead from right to left. Thread one 8mm faceted bead and repeat beading pattern five more times. Thread wire through first 8mm faceted bead to form circle. Twist tail tightly around wire close to bead; trim tail.

Fig. D1

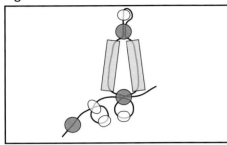

2. For center, refer to Fig. D2 and thread wire through each pebble bead to complete inner circle. Thread wire through first pebble bead and wrap around inner circle wire to secure. For center anchor, bring wire across center to opposite side, loop around inner circle wire between two pebble beads. Thread wire through one 12mm melon and one pebble bead. Double back through melon bead, using pliers to bend wire close to pebble bead. Bring wire back to starting point on inner circle wire.

Fig. D2

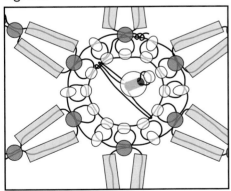

3. With back of ornament facing up, refer to Fig. D3 and twist wire around center wire behind melon bead. Loop wire between two pebble beads on side, perpendicular to anchor wire. Loop wire around inner circle wire on opposite side. Return to center and twist wire tightly around anchor wire, behind melon bead; trim tail.

Fig. D3

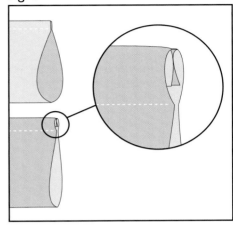

4. For hanger, attach a 6" loop of wire on outer circle between two spokes.

SWIRLED GLASS ICICLES
(Shown on page 44)

To create our Swirled Glass Icicles, begin with a 7 1/2"-long clear glass icicle ornament. Holding the icicle on its side, apply a line of craft glue along one raised edge. Press silver seed beads into the glue with your fingers and allow to dry before repeating along each remaining swirl.

BEADED GIFT BAGS
(Shown on pages 43 and 45)

For each bag, you will need 1/2 yd. sheer fabric, 15mm bugle beads, crystal seed beads, 4mm faceted crystal beads, 5mm opalescent glass beads, beading needle, beaded trim with a flange, 20" length of white rattail cord, and a 24" length of silver miniature garland.

Use a 1/4" seam allowance for all sewing, unless otherwise indicated.

1. Cut an 11" x 17" piece of fabric. For star placement, measure up 3 3/4" from center bottom of one 11" side and lightly mark center point. Referring to Beading Diagram at right, begin beading at bottom spoke of star. To keep threads from showing through sheer fabric, run threads back through beads when moving from one spoke to the next.

2. To make a French seam, matching wrong sides and long raw edges fold fabric in half (star will be on outside). Sew seam, forming a tube. Turn tube wrong side out (star will be on the inside) and finger press seam to one side. Sew second seam to encase first seam (Fig. 1).

Fig. 1

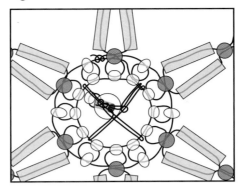

3. To form bottom of bag, keep star to the inside and turn tube right side out until raw edges meet. Leaving tube open, baste around raw edges. With seam at center back and edge of trim flange even with raw edges of fabric, insert trim between fabric layers; using a seam allowance equal to the width of flange, sew bottom closed. Trim seam allowance to 1/4"w and zigzag over raw edges; turn bag to right side.

4. Place gift in bag. To close bag, tie rattail cord and garland into a half loop bow around top.

BEADING DIAGRAM

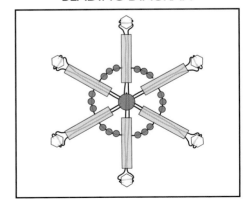

BEADING BASICS

BEADING TIPS

Refer to the project supply list for each project to identify the types of beads and other supplies that we used to create our ornaments and gift bags.

To develop the different styles of ornaments, we chose beads from several manufacturers. The supply list that accompanies each project includes the size and number of most beads.

For designs where a certain size bead is needed to complete the project, such as beaded collars, use the same size beads as listed in the supply list, or adjust the number of beads as needed to complete the ornament.

We found that with some types of beads, such as "E" and seed beads, sizes may vary within a package, and the number of beads may need to be adjusted.

Place beads on a paper plate, bowl, or chamois cloth, or use the sticky side of several self-adhesive notes stuck together (to prevent them from curling). To keep from dropping beads, thread beads directly from the plate onto needle or wire.

Pick up several beads on needle before moving them onto the thread. With practice, this is a real time-saver, too.

To hold ornament steady when working with beaded collars or other ball ornament designs, place ornament in a paper cup.

BEADING WITH THREAD

Choose from a variety of beading needles and threads to create beautiful collars and to bead on fabric. We recommend that you work with beading thread, which is stronger than sewing thread. Be sure to use a size needle and thread that will pass through the smallest bead used for your ornament without putting stress on the thread.

Threading Needle

Thread beading needle with one doubled strand of thread unless otherwise indicated in project instructions. It may be helpful to tape the tail to a table as you begin threading beads.

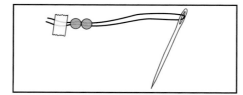

Locking Bead

A locking bead at the beginning of a strand keeps the beads from sliding off your thread. Leaving a 3" tail, string first bead on thread. Pass needle around and through bead again to lock in place. Thread beads as indicated in project instructions. Locking beads are also used at the end of a thread or dangle.

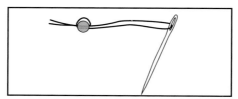

Securing Thread Ends

To secure an ending thread, lock last bead in place and double back through last four beads; unthread needle, leaving a tail. Add new thread to continue strand (see below), or trim tail and dot locking bead and thread end with liquid fray preventative; allow to dry.

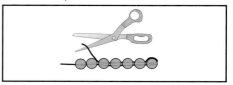

To secure a beginning thread, rethread needle with beginning tail. Pass needle around locking bead and through next four beads. Trim tail and dot locking bead and thread end with liquid fray preventative; allow to dry.

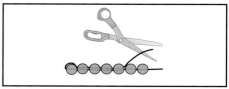

Adding Threads

To add thread, pass newly threaded needle through the last three beads on the strand, leaving a 3" tail. Thread needle through last bead twice to lock in place and continue beading. Trim tails and dot locking bead and thread ends with liquid fray preventative; allow to dry.

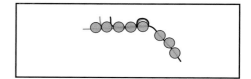

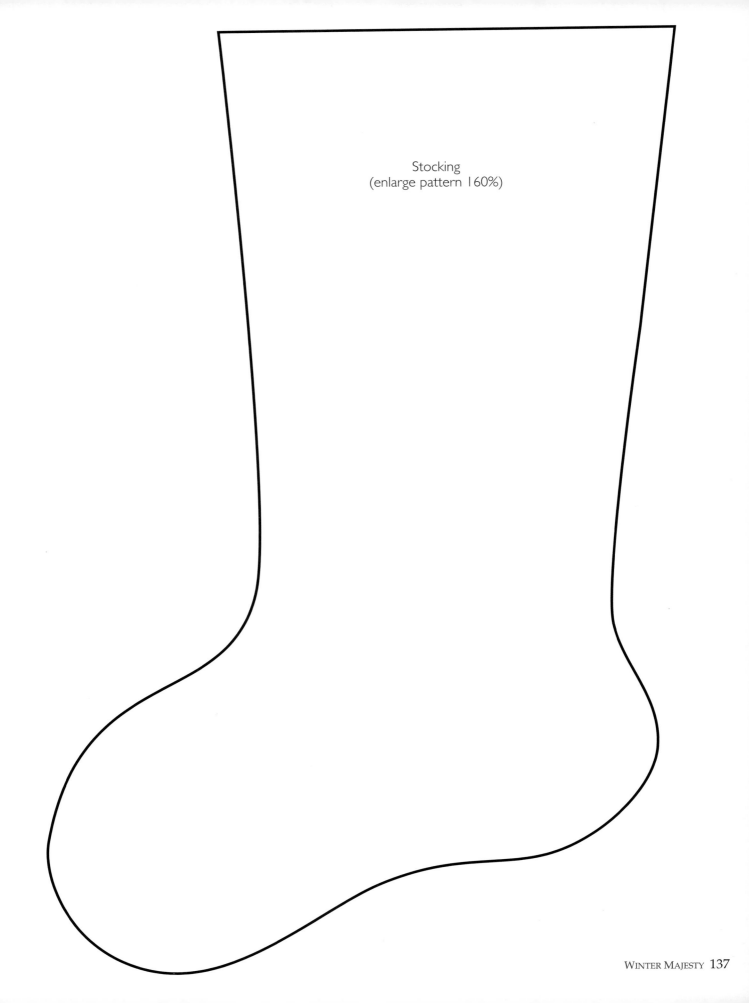

Stocking
(enlarge pattern 160%)

Flea Market Fancies

FIREPLACE ENSEMBLE
(Shown on page 52)

You will need a vintage Christmas-motif tablecloth, $\frac{1}{2}$"w paper-backed fusible web tape, fabric glue, rickrack, purchased cardboard fireplace screen (we used a Create-A-Room™ fireplace cover kit), felt to coordinate with tablecloth, hot glue gun, kraft paper, fabric to coordinate with tablecloth, paper-backed fusible web, and a pressing cloth.

Find a tablecloth large enough to make a scarf accommodating the desired width and drop-length for your mantel and to cut assorted pieces to cover a fireplace screen.

MANTEL SCARF

1. For scarf, measure depth of mantel and add desired number of inches for drop (our drop measures 13"); cut a strip from one end of tablecloth the determined measurement. Set remainder of tablecloth aside for fireplace screen.
2. Use web tape to hem raw edges of scarf. Glue rickrack along side and bottom edges of scarf; allow to dry. Place scarf on mantel.

FIREPLACE SCREEN

1. To cover screen, leave at least 2" between shapes and draw around screen twice on wrong side of felt; cut out one shape 2" outside drawn line for front of screen and cut out remaining shape $\frac{1}{2}$" inside drawn line for back of screen. Center right side of screen on front felt piece. Clipping and easing as necessary, hot glue edges of felt to back of screen. Center and glue back felt piece to back of screen.

2. For front of screen, glue rickrack 1" inside edges of center and side panels.
3. To make a pattern for each side panel, draw 1" inside rickrack on kraft paper and cut out. Use pattern to cut two shapes from coordinating fabric. Clipping and easing as necessary, use web tape to hem edges of shapes. Glue fabric panels to centers of side panels.
4. Fuse web to wrong side of remainder of tablecloth. Cutting just outside edges, cut desired motifs from tablecloth piece; remove paper backing.
5. Arrange motifs on front of screen as desired; using pressing cloth, fuse in place.

If you don't have enough of a favorite linen to make both a Mantel Scarf and a Fireplace Screen, simply sew the border from one edge of the tablecloth onto a coordinating fabric piece and size or fold to fit your mantel. Use the remaining fabric motifs for your screen.

STARRY TREE TOPPER
(Shown on page 52)

You will need a hot glue gun, red and silver jumbo rickrack, aluminum star-shaped gelatin mold (we used a 5" dia. mold), 1" dia. off-white and $\frac{3}{4}$" dia. red buttons, scrap of red felt, pinking shears, aluminum tube pan with fluted sides (we used a 9$\frac{1}{4}$" dia. pan), medium rickrack with print motif, wire cutters, 14- and 26-gauge craft wire, pliers, and a string of decorative miniature lights (our string has twenty bulbs).

1. For star, glue red rickrack along inside rim of star mold. Glue off-white

button to center of felt scrap; use pinking shears to trim felt just outside edges of button. Glue red button to center of off-white button; glue felt to center bottom of mold.
2. For pan, glue silver rickrack along inside top edges of tube pan; glue print rickrack to pan just below silver rickrack.
3. Measure height of tube; add 4". Cut two lengths of 14-gauge wire the determined measurement. Bend each wire length into a U shape; insert ends of each U through tube, from bottom to top. Bend 1" of each wire end tightly over top edge of tube.
4. (*Note*: Refer to Lights Diagram for Steps 4 and 5.) Beginning with free end of light string, thread and pull string through center of tube pan until all lights are at front of tube. Leaving a 2" tail, wrap one end of a 24" length of 26-gauge wire snugly around bottom of first bulb on string. Place next bulb on string close to first bulb and secure in place with wire; continue action until each bulb is secured in place leaving a 2" wire tail after last bulb.
5. Thread another 24" length of 26-gauge wire through excess cord below bulbs. With bulbs facing toward bottom of pan, place lights over tube; twist wire ends together at top and bottom to secure around tube.
6. Glue inside bottom of star mold to tube, covering wire.

LIGHTS DIAGRAM

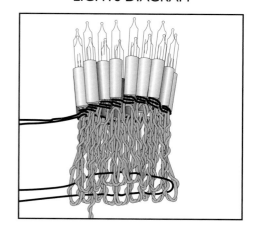

WINDOW FRAME
(Shown on page 54)

You will need wood glue, decorative wooden cutout, wooden window frame, sandpaper, tack cloth, acrylic paint, paintbrush, clear acrylic sealer, felt, corrugated cardboard, fabric, photographs, photo spray mount, flathead screws, screwdriver, two eye screws, and picture hanging wire.

Allow glue, paint, and sealer to dry after each application.

1. Use wood glue to adhere wooden cutout to center top of window frame. Lightly sand then wipe with tack cloth. Paint frame; apply two coats of sealer.
2. For photo board, measure height and width of opening in frame and add 1" to each measurement. Cut felt and cardboard the determined measurements. Cut a piece of fabric 2" larger on each side than cardboard piece.
3. Center cardboard on wrong side of fabric; fold and glue fabric edges to the back of cardboard.
4. Arrange photos on board; follow spray mount manufacturer's instructions to adhere photos to board.
5. Attach photo board to back of frame with screws. Glue felt to back of photo board. To hang frame, twist eye screws into wood on each side of back of frame. Run wire between eye screws, twisting around itself to secure.

If you have cherished vintage photographs that you would like to use in your projects, consider having copies made so you can preserve your original print. Some of the many options available include self-service photo processors, computer scanning and printing, black and white or color photocopying, and professional photographic reproduction. Check with your local photofinisher for other suggestions.

COLLECTIBLE MOLD ORNAMENTS
(Shown on page 53)

You will need assorted colors of baby and medium rickrack, silicone adhesive, aluminum molds, assorted buttons, scraps of felt, and pinking shears.

Use silicone adhesive for all gluing; allow adhesive to dry after each application.

1. For each ornament with hanger, cut a 6" length of rickrack; glue ends to top or inside top of mold. To make a three-dimensional ornament, glue two molds together with the same size openings.
2. To decorate each ornament, glue lengths of rickrack along edges of mold. If desired, glue buttons to mold or glue a button to center of a felt scrap and use pinking shears to cut around felt just outside edges of button; glue felt to mold.

To make temporary decorative additions to objects such as our Collectible Mold Ornaments, adhere embellishments with clear silicone household adhesive. When the adhesive is dry, the decorations can be removed without damaging your items, leaving them ready to use or embellish again!

To preserve your collection of photographs, wear cotton gloves while handling them to reduce the damage caused by oils and acid in fingerprints. Clean the surface of photographs before storage or display by using a soft, dry paintbrush. Store all of your photographs in acid-free paper or clear uncoated Mylar or polyethylene envelopes in a cool, dry environment away from direct light.

VINTAGE TABLECLOTH TREE SKIRT
(Shown on page 54)

You will need a vintage Christmas-motif rectangular tablecloth (ours measures 52" x 66"), fabric marking pencil, drawing compass, single-fold white bias binding, and four 24" lengths of $5/8$"w red grosgrain ribbon.

1. To fold tablecloth into a square for skirt, mark center of tablecloth and center of edges on both long sides. Make a pleat on either side of center mark by folding tablecloth up to center mark until square; pin in place (Fig. 1).

Fig. 1

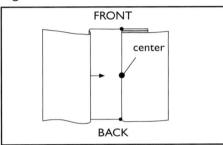

2. Use compass to draw a 5" dia. circle around center mark. Draw a straight line to connect center back edge mark to center mark. Being careful not to cut top layers of pleat, cut an opening in tablecloth along drawn line; cutting through all layers at center, cut away circle along drawn line (Fig. 2).

Fig. 2

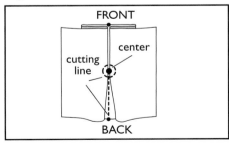

3. Stitch binding over raw edges of center back opening and center circle. Press pleats, then remove pins.
4. Gather each corner of skirt with a length of ribbon tied into a bow.

BOLSTER PILLOW
(Shown on page 55)

You will need a bolster pillow form (ours measures 16"-long), vintage Christmas-motif tablecloth, 1/2"w paper-backed fusible web tape, two rubber bands, and two 18" lengths of 1/2"w satin ribbon.

Use a 1/2" seam allowance for all sewing.

1. For pillow cover, measure length of pillow form and add 6"; measure circumference and add 1". Cut a piece of tablecloth the determined measurements.
2. Use web tape to hem short edges of cover. Matching right sides and raw edges, sew long edges together. Turn cover right-side out and insert pillow form.
3. Use rubber bands to gather ends of cover close to pillow; cover rubber bands with ribbon lengths tied into bows.

SQUARE PILLOW
(Shown on page 55)

You will need a square pillow form (ours measures 14"), tissue paper, vintage Christmas-motif tablecloth, and 1 1/2 yds. of fringed trim.

Use a 1/2" seam allowance for all sewing.

1. For pillow, measure across pillow form; add 1". Cut a square pattern from tissue paper the determined measurements. Lay pattern on right side of tablecloth to "view" desired placement of motifs for pillow front. Pin in place; cut out pillow front. Use pattern to cut pillow back from tablecloth.
2. With right sides together and leaving bottom edge open for turning and inserting pillow form, sew front and back together, rounding corners. Clip curves, then turn right-side out. Insert pillow form; sew opening closed.
3. Turning under raw ends, whipstitch fringe along edges of pillow.

ROUND PILLOW
(Shown on page 55)

You will need two 15" squares cut from a vintage tablecloth (we used a white damask cloth), string, fabric marking pencil, thumbtack, polyester fiberfill, 3 1/2 yds. of rickrack, ribbon rose, and a vintage potholder.

Use a 1/2" seam allowance for all sewing.

1. For pillow front and back, fold each fabric square in half, then fold in half again. Tie one end of string to pencil. Insert thumbtack through string 7 1/2" from pencil for cutting line. Insert thumbtack through fabric as shown in Fig. 1; mark outer line. Cut along drawn line through all fabric layers.

Fig. 1

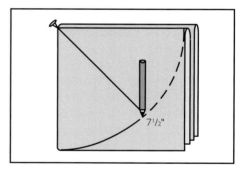

7 1/2"

2. Matching right sides and leaving an opening for turning, sew circles together along outside edges; clip edges every 1/2". Turn right side-out and press. Stuff pillow with fiberfill; Sew opening closed.
3. Securing ends at center front, wrap four 30" lengths of rickrack around pillow; tack rickrack at center back and side seams. Tack rose to center of potholder. Covering ends of rickrack, tack potholder to center front of pillow.

Household linens are little luxuries that never go out of style, whether they're handed down through the family or purchased at a flea market or secondhand shop. The vintage pieces are ideal for creating decorative accents throughout your home, especially for the Christmas season. These wonderful and plentiful old prints can become the focus of your Christmas décor.

Those in perfect condition can be used for their original purpose, but those with slight imperfections from years of use — such as stains or tears — are usable, too. Simply mask the damaged area by folding, pleating, hemming, or cutting away — or you could place greenery, ornaments, pinecones, or garlands over the damaged area.

The Sharing of Christmas

DÉCOUPAGED CLOCK
(Shown on page 58)

You will need wood glue; small wooden turning for finial; wooden clock, (ours measures 6¹/₂"w x 10"h); sandpaper; primer; red and green acrylic paint; paintbrushes; clear acrylic spray sealer; tracing paper; design cut from old Christmas card (large enough to cover area behind clock movements and small enough to allow room for phrase); tape; transfer paper; stylus; black fine-point permanent marker; découpage glue; hot glue gun, star-shaped buttons; and a battery clock movements kit to fit clock.

Allow wood glue, primer, paint, sealer, and découpage glue to dry after each application.

1. Use wood glue to attach finial to top of clock.
2. Sand, then prime clock.
3. Paint clock with two coats of red, then apply sealer to clock. Paint clock with two coats of green. Lightly sand clock to create an aged look, revealing the red basecoat.
4. Trace "Time To Rejoice" pattern, below, onto tracing paper. Spacing as desired and centering card design over hole for clock movements, position phrase and design on clock; use tape to hold phrase in place. Remove design from clock.
5. Use transfer paper and stylus to transfer phrase to clock. Paint phrase red, then outline with marker.
6. Apply sealer to front and back of cutout. Following manufacturer's instructions, découpage card design to clock, then seal entire clock with découpage glue.
7. Hot glue buttons to clock.
8. Follow manufacturer's instructions to attach clock movements to clock.

"JOY" CANDLEHOLDER
(Shown on page 58)

You will need assorted colors of acrylic paint (we used red, yellow, light green, and green paint), paintbrushes, unfinished wooden candleholder (ours measures 6"h x 3" dia.), tracing paper, transfer paper, stylus, black fine-point paint pen, and clear acrylic sealer.

Refer to Painting Techniques, page 151, before beginning project. Allow paint, paint pen, and sealer to dry after each application.

1. Paint basecoats on candleholders.
2. Trace star pattern, below, onto tracing paper. Use transfer paper and stylus to transfer design to candleholder.
3. Paint star and details on candleholder (we painted various sizes of dots and straight and curly lines).
4. Use paint pen to outline star and write "JOY" in center. Draw accent lines between paint colors.
5. Apply two coats of sealer to candleholder.

Note: Enlarge or reduce pattern to fit on your clock before tracing pattern.

ANGEL FLOWERPOT TREE
(Shown on page 59)

You will need brown, green, ivory, metallic gold, flesh, and pink acrylic paint; paintbrushes; $3^1/2$"h x 15" dia. terra-cotta saucer; one each 12"h x 13" dia., $8^1/2$"h x 9" dia., 6"h x 7" dia., $5^1/2$"h x $4^1/2$" dia., and 3"h x 3" dia. terra-cotta flowerpots; two sizes of flat-backed papier-mâché star ornaments; $2^1/2$" dia. papier-mâché ball; wooden doll pin stand; matte clear acrylic spray sealer; metallic gold medium-point marker; black fine-point permanent marker; craft glue; doll hair; small star garland; hot glue gun; $30^1/2$" length of $1/2$" dia. dowel; $9^1/2$"w grapevine bow for wings; grapevine garland; and berry garland.

The saucer and flowerpots are all used upside-down for this project. Use craft glue for all gluing unless otherwise indicated. Allow paint, sealer, and craft glue to dry after each application.

1. Applying at least three coats of paint, paint saucer brown, three largest pots green, remaining two pots ivory, and stars gold; paint papier-mâché ball (head) and pin stand (neck) flesh. Apply two coats of sealer to all items.
2. Use a pencil to lightly draw angel's arms, hands, cuffs, collar, and buttons on smallest pot for top of dress. Paint hands flesh. Excluding hands, use gold marker to paint over drawn lines, color rim of pot, cuffs, and collar and to draw designs on remaining ivory pot for bottom of dress.
3. Use black marker to draw eyes and mouth on head and to outline hands; use fingertip to lightly dab pink paint on face for cheeks.
4. Arrange and glue hair on head; glue head to neck. Shape star garland into a halo on top of head and, using hot glue, spot glue in place. Glue neck to center bottom of dress bodice (smallest pot).

5. Stack all but smallest pot in graduated sizes on saucer. Insert dowel through center holes in pots. Place angel head and bodice on top of stack. Glue wings to back of angel.
6. Soak grapevine garland in water until pliable. Using hot glue and spot gluing as necessary, spiral grapevine garland around tree, then berry garland along grapevine garland.
7. Cut hangers from large star ornaments; hot glue large stars to pots and hang smaller stars along garland as desired.

CARD AND PHOTO DISPLAY
(Shown on page 60)

You will need a plastic terra-cotta-look planter, off-white acrylic paint, paintbrush, clear acrylic spray sealer, hot glue gun, wide ribbon, floral foam block cut to fit snugly in planter, fresh greenery (some with berries), Christmas ornaments, silver 20-gauge craft wire, wire cutters, and needle-nose pliers.

Cut wire in varying lengths to stagger heights of holders for cards.

1. *Dry Brush,* page 152, planter with off-white paint; allow to dry. Lightly apply sealer to planter.
2. Overlapping ends at front, glue a length of ribbon around planter; make, then glue a bow to overlap.
3. Soak floral foam in water and place in planter. Arrange greenery and ornaments in planter.
4. For each tree-shaped cardholder, cut a 24"-long piece of wire. Holding wire at center (bottom of tree) with pliers, form tree shape from bottom to top and back to bottom; wrap wire around itself to secure. Form end of wire into a tight spiral behind tree; cut away excess wire. Insert cardholder into foam.
5. For each spiraled cardholder, cut a 24"-long piece of wire. Holding wire at center, form wire into a tight spiral; cut away excess wire. Insert spiral into foam.

NAPKIN PRESS
(Shown on page 60)

You will need a 26" square of pre-quilted fabric, 28" square of flannel fabric, disappearing fabric marker or chalk pencil, $17^3/4$" square of cardboard, $1/4$"w paper-backed fusible web tape, four $5/8$" dia. buttons, embroidery floss, and $3/8$"w ribbon.

1. With wrong sides together, center and pin quilted fabric on top of flannel fabric, with edges of flannel extending 1" beyond quilted fabric on all sides. Make a mark at center edge of each side of flannel. Lightly draw a straight line from each mark, making a square in a square (Fig. 1). Sew along lines around three sides, forming a pocket; insert cardboard piece and sew last side closed.

Fig. 1

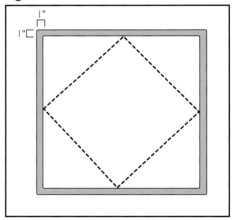

2. Pin and sew though all fabric layers close to outer edge of quilted fabric. Trim each corner of flannel, leaving a $1/4$" seam allowance. Press seam allowance over corner; press flannel under $1/2$" on all sides to form hem. Following manufacturer's instructions, apply fusible web to hem. Turn hem over raw edges of quilted fabric, miter corners, and press in place.
3. For ties, use embroidery floss to sew on buttons and a 10" length of ribbon to each corner of press.

BEADED CHARMS

(Shown on page 61)

For each charm, you will need nylon-coated jewelry wire, wire cutters, one clasp and eyelet, needle-nose pliers, 1"-long eye pins, assorted beads (we used a variety of $^1/_8$" to $^5/_8$" glass, tube, pony, and seed beads).

1. For each charm, cut an 8" length of wire; leaving a 1"-long tail, thread one end of wire through small hole in eyelet twice and twist to secure.
2. For each dangle, thread assorted beads onto an eye pin; crimp bottom of pin to secure. Repeat to make fourteen dangles.
3. Beginning with a bead and alternating beads and dangles, thread thirteen beads and twelve dangles onto wire.
4. Leaving a 1" tail, wrap remaining end of wire through hole in clasp and twist to secure. Thread each tail back through beads and eye pins on wire; trim any excess wire.
5. Attach one dangle to each hole in eyelet.

HAND-PAINTED CERAMIC PLATE

(Shown on page 61)

You will need tracing paper, graphite transfer paper, stylus, greenware dinner plate (cleaned), assorted ceramic underglaze paints, paintbrushes, and clear ceramic glaze.

Handle greenware gently, as it breaks easily. Use very light pressure when transferring designs to plate to prevent making hard indentions in greenware. Follow manufacturer's instructions to paint designs on greenware and to apply glaze to bisqueware.

1. Trace snowman, leaf, flower, and star patterns, page 150, onto tracing paper. Using transfer paper and stylus, transfer snowman to center of plate; repeating as desired, transfer leaf, flower, and star patterns around rim of plate, freehanding squiggle lines between designs. Personalize banner as desired.
2. Using underglazes, paint designs on plate, then outline and add highlights to painted areas as desired. Use end of paintbrush to paint dots on plate. If desired, add your "signature" and date on back of plate.
3. Have painted greenware plate fired to bisque. Apply glaze to bisque plate; have plate fired again.

HAT AND SCARF

(Shown on page 62)

You will need white and green polyester fleece, fleece hat and scarf, 1"w satin ribbon, three shank buttons, and chenille cord.

Refer to Embroidery Stitches, page 154, before beginning project.

1. For each flower, cut a strip of fleece $1^3/_4$"w × 15"-long. Sew short ends together to form a circle. Using a *Running Stitch*, work a 1"w zigzag pattern through center of strip (Fig. 1). As you stitch, gently draw thread up until circle forms flower shape; knot to secure. Tack flowers to hat and scarf.

Fig. 1

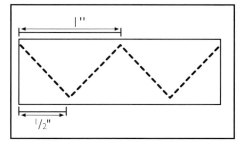

2. For flower center, fold a 7" length of ribbon in half, matching selvage edges. Sew *Running Stitches* along selvage edges, gathering ribbon into a tight circle. Sew ends together and knot to secure. Insert button shank through flower center, then place on top of flower; sew in place.
3. For each leaf, cut a 1"w × 7"-long strip of fleece. Sew *Running Stitches* along one long edge of strip, gathering strip into a circle. Sew ends together and knot to secure. Arrange leaves close to flowers and tack in place, allowing fleece to fold over, forming a leaf shape.
4. For stems, use thread to *Couch* lengths of chenille cord around flowers and leaves.

You can find all your ceramic supplies at a ceramic shop, including greenware, paints, and glazes. Ask the ceramic experts at the shop for help in selecting, cleaning, and painting your greenware plate. The ceramic shop will fire your plate for a small fee. Following our instructions, your plate will need to be fired twice; from greenware to bisque, then again to glaze it.

As an option, there are also "Do It Yourself" ceramic stores that offer already cleaned and fired bisqueware — ready to paint (instead of greenware). The plate can be made following the same instructions and most of these stores will glaze and fire your piece for you after you have painted it.

FLEECE-TRIMMED JACKET
(Shown on page 63)

You will need a jacket with a collar, long sleeves, and pockets; and animal print polyester fleece.

Use ¹/₂" seam allowance for all sewing.

1. To cover jacket collar, measure collar; add one inch to all sides and double the width measurement. Cut a piece of fleece the determined measurements. Matching right sides and long edges, fold fabric in half and sew short ends together; turn to right side. Slip cover onto collar, fold raw edges under ¹/₂", and hand stitch in place.
2. For 4"w cuffs, cut two pieces of fleece 9"w by the circumference of the sleeve plus 1". Matching right sides and 9"w edges, fold fabric in half and sew ends together, forming a circle. Turn to right side. Matching wrong sides and raw edges, fold in half. Slip cuff into end of sleeve, keeping raw edges of cuff even with sleeve end; stitch in place then fold cuff up over end of sleeve.
3. Measure pocket; cut two pieces fleece this measurement and hand stitch in place over pocket (if your jacket has a slit-style pocket, measure width of opening, cut fleece this measurement by 4"h, and stitch in place, on jacket front to create a false pocket front).

Adding your own embellishments can transform ordinary items into one-of-a-kind gifts that will be treasured forever. Add beads, buttons, or trims to linens and clothing — découpage, stencil, or stamp holiday motifs on plain wooden frames, glassware, or pottery to make unique presents.

RUBBER STAMP SOAPS AND GIFT TAGS
(Shown on page 64)

You will need green and white card stock, decorative-edge craft scissors, craft glue, rubber stamp to fit in mold (we used a 1¹/₂" star), green ink pad, rubber cement, soap mold (we used a 2¹/₂" dia. round mold), candle mold release spray, clear glycerin soap bricks, soap dye, soap fragrance, clear cellophane, and red raffia.

1. For each tag, cut a 2¹/₂" × 5" piece of green card stock and fold in half lengthwise. Use decorative-edge scissors to cut a 1³/₄" square of white card stock. Stamp design on square, then center and glue to tag.
2. Remove stamp from block. With the side that was attached to the block facing down, use rubber cement to adhere stamp to the inside bottom of soap mold; allow to dry. Spray mold and stamp with mold release.
3. Following manufacturer's instructions, melt glycerin soap brick; add dye and fragrance to melted soap as desired.
4. For each bar, pour melted soap into mold; allow to harden, then remove soap. Repeat for desired number of bars. Remove stamp from mold. Use rubber cement to reattach stamp to block if desired; allow to dry.
5. Wrap soap in cellophane; tie with a length of raffia.

HOLIDAY HAND TOWELS
(Shown on page 64)

For each towel, you will need a hand towel, ¹/₄" dia. twisted cord with a ¹/₂" flange, 1"w grosgrain ribbon, two coordinating colors of jumbo rickrack, and buttons.

1. For towel with buttons below trim, measure width of towel and add 1". Cut two lengths of cord, one length of ribbon, and one length of each color rickrack the determined measurement.
2. Press raw ends of cord and ribbon ¹/₂" to wrong side. With flange edges touching, pin cord lengths along edge of towel; sew in place. Sew ribbon over flange. Twist lengths of rickrack together; press raw edges ¹/₂" to wrong side and sew along center of ribbon.
3. Spacing evenly, sew buttons to towel below trim.
4. For towel with buttons above trim, measure width of towel and add 2". Cut a length of cord, and each color of rickrack, the determined measurement.
5. Press raw edges of cord ¹/₂" to wrong side. With raw edges wrapping to the back of towel, pin, then sew cord in a wavy line along one edge of towel. Twist lengths of rickrack together; press raw edges ¹/₂" to wrong side and sew over flange.
6. Spacing evenly, sew buttons to towel above trim.

APPLIQUÉD THROW
(Shown on page 65)

You will need tracing paper, assorted colors of felt, polyester fleece throw (ours measured 50"w x 70"-long), assorted colors of embroidery floss, white ³/₄" dia. pom-pom, and a red colored pencil.

Refer to Making Patterns, page 151, and Embroidery Stitches, page 154, before beginning project. Use three strands of floss unless otherwise indicated.

1. Trace patterns, pages 145 – 149, onto tracing paper; cut out. Use patterns to cut shapes from felt.
2. Arrange and pin shapes to one corner of throw. Work *Blanket Stitches* along edges of coat, boots, and bag. Work uneven *Straight Stitches* along edges of beard, stars, tree, and to make snowflakes on tree. Work long *Overcast Stitches* along edges of staff. Work a *French Knot* for eye.
3. Tack pom-pom to top of hat. Use colored pencil to color cheek.

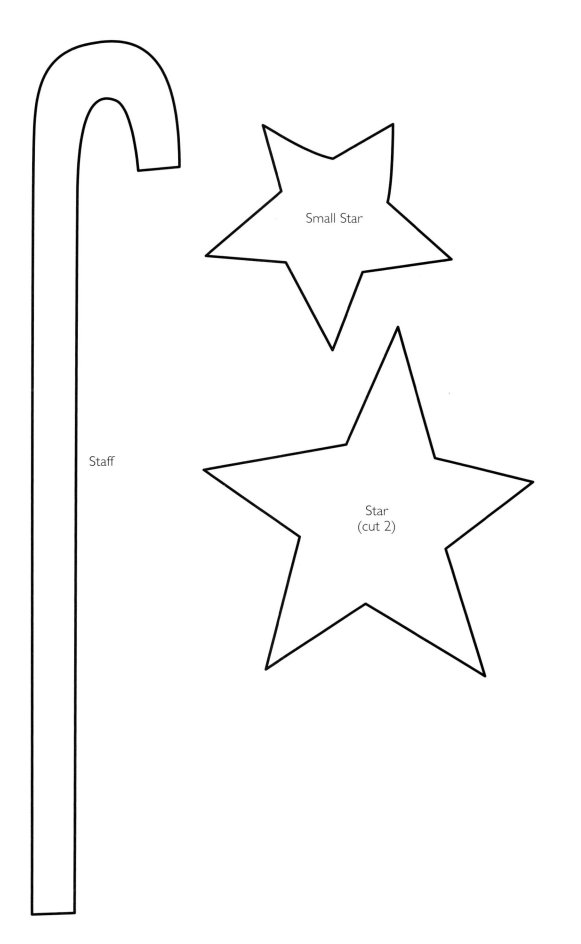

Staff

Small Star

Star
(cut 2)

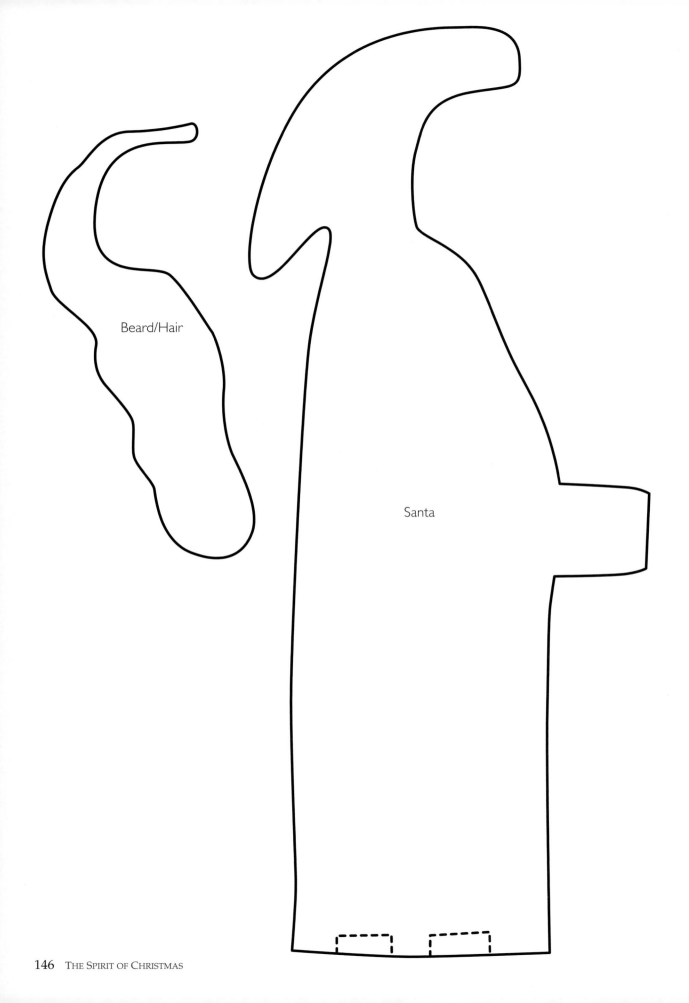

Beard/Hair

Santa

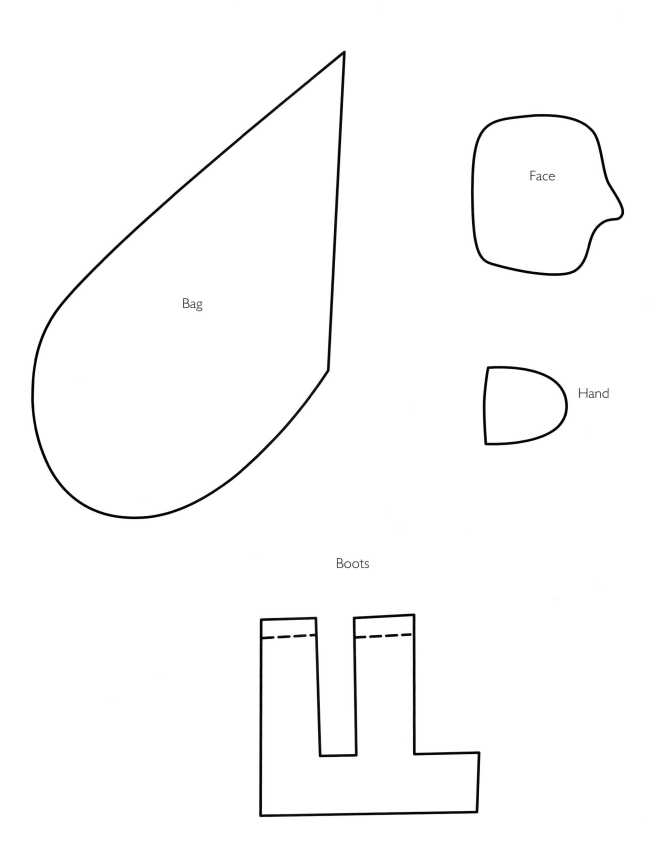

Bag

Face

Hand

Boots

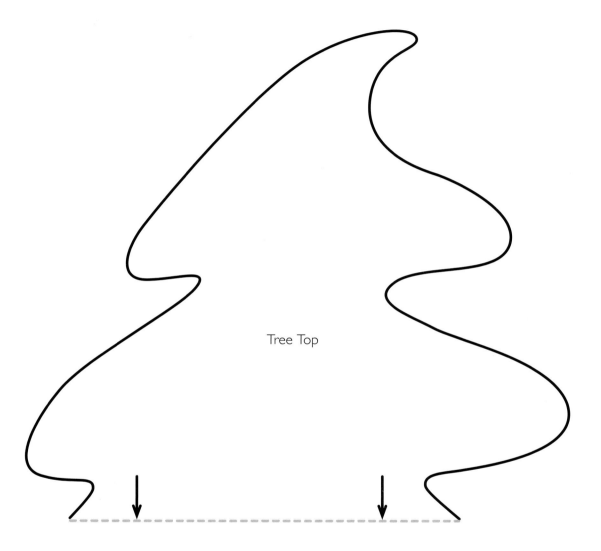

Tree Top

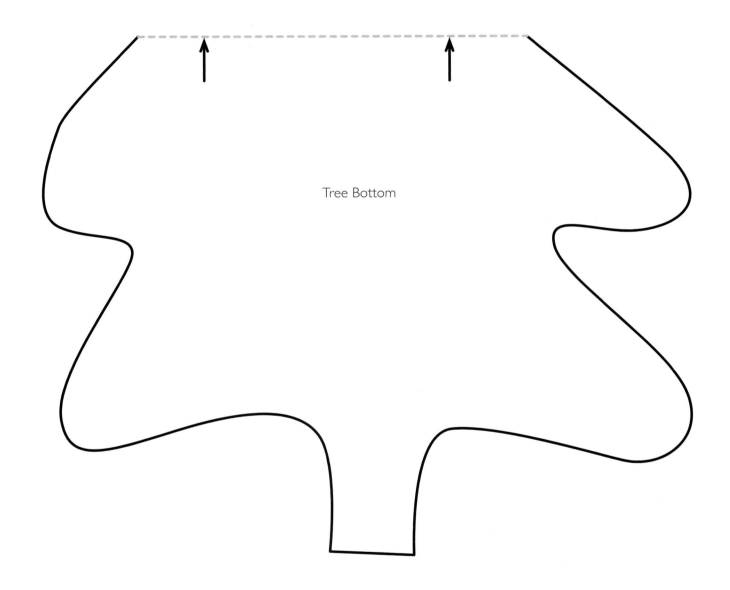

Tree Bottom

Snowman

Leaf

Star

Leaf

Flower

ADHESIVES

When using any adhesive, carefully follow the manufacturer's instructions.

White craft glue:
Recommended for paper. Dry flat.

Tacky craft glue:
Recommended for paper, fabric, florals, or wood. Dry flat or secure items with clothespins or straight pins until glue is dry.

Craft glue stick:
Recommended for paper or for gluing small, lightweight items to paper or other surfaces. Dry flat.

Fabric glue:
Recommended for fabric or paper. Dry flat or secure items with clothespins or straight pins until glue is dry.

Découpage glue:
Recommended for découpaging fabric or paper to a surface such as wood or glass. Use purchased découpage glue or mix one part craft glue with one part water.

Hot or low-temperature glue gun:
Recommended for paper, fabric, florals, or wood. Hold in place until set.

Rubber cement:
Recommended for paper and cardboard. May discolor photos; may discolor paper with age. Dry flat (dries very quickly).

Spray adhesive:
Recommended for paper or fabric. Can be repositioned or permanent. Dry flat.

Household cement:
Recommended for ceramic or metal. Secure items with clothespins until glue is dry.

Wood glue:
Recommended for wood. Nail, screw, or clamp items together until glue is dry.

Silicone adhesive:
Recommended for ceramic, glass, leather, rubber, wood, and plastics. Forms a flexible and waterproof bond.

MAKING PATTERNS

When entire pattern is shown, place tracing paper over pattern and trace pattern. For a more durable pattern, use a permanent marker to trace pattern onto stencil plastic.

When pattern pieces are stacked or overlapped, place tracing paper over pattern and follow a single color to trace pattern. Repeat to trace each pattern separately onto tracing paper.

When tracing a two-part pattern, match dashed lines and arrows to trace the pattern onto tracing paper.

When only half of pattern is shown (indicated by a solid blue line on pattern), fold tracing paper in half. Place the fold along solid blue line and trace pattern half. Place fold of pattern along fold in fabric.

PAINTING TECHNIQUES

A disposable foam plate makes a good palette for holding and mixing paint colors. It can easily be placed in a large resealable plastic bag to keep remaining paint wet while waiting for an area of applied paint to dry.

As well, when waiting for a large area to dry before applying a second coat, wrap your paintbrushes in plastic wrap and place in the refrigerator to keep paint from drying on your brushes. Always clean brushes thoroughly after use to keep them in good condition.

Following manufacturer's instructions will produce the best results for any paint product. If you are unfamiliar with a specific painting technique, practice on a scrap of wood, cardboard or paper before beginning project.

Work in a well-ventilated area and protect work surfaces with newspaper or a drop cloth.

PREPARING PROJECT FOR PAINTING

Remove any hardware and set aside. Repair any problems, such as holes, cracks, and other imperfections, as desired. Sand item and wipe with tack cloth. Apply primer and allow to dry. Paint project according to instructions. Clean hardware and re-attach or replace with new hardware.

TIPS FOR PAINTING ON FABRIC

If painting on fabric or a garment, wash, dry, and press item according to paint manufacturer's recommendations. To help stabilize fabric, insert a T-shirt form into a garment, pin fabric to a piece of foam core, or iron shiny side of freezer paper to wrong side of item under area to be painted. After painting, allow to dry before removing freezer paper.

TRANSFERRING PATTERNS

Trace pattern onto tracing paper. Using removable tape, tape pattern to project. Place transfer paper, coated side down, between project and tracing paper. If transferring pattern onto a dark surface, use light-colored transfer paper to transfer pattern. Use a stylus or pencil to lightly draw over pattern lines onto project.

TRANSFERRING DETAILS

To transfer detail lines to design, reposition pattern and transfer paper over painted basecoat and use a stylus or pencil to lightly draw over detail lines of design onto project.

PAINTING BASECOATS

A basecoat is a solid color of paint that covers the project's entire surface or one or more colors that cover selected areas of a project's surface.

Use a medium to large paintbrush for large areas and a small brush for small areas. Do not overload brush. Allow paint to dry after each coat.

ADDING DETAILS

Use a permanent marker or paint pen to draw over transferred detail lines or to create freehanded details on project.

AGED FINISHES

This technique creates a faux-aged finish.

Allowing to dry after each application, paint project the desired basecoat color. Randomly apply a thin layer of paste floor wax with a soft cloth or rub a candle over areas on project to be aged (such as the edges). Paint project the desired top coat color and allow to dry. Lightly sand project to remove some of the paint, revealing the basecoat color in some areas. Wipe project with a tack cloth to remove dust, then seal with a clear acrylic sealer.

"C" STROKE

Dip an angle or flat paintbrush in paint. Touch tip to surface, pulling brush to the right or left. Pull brush toward you while applying pressure. When stroke is desired length, lift brush gradually while pulling to the opposite direction to form the tail of the stroke.

COMMA STROKE

Dip round brush into water; blot on paper towel. Dip brush into paint; touch brush tip to painting surface. Apply slight pressure to brush to spread out brush hairs. Pull brush to the right or left in a curve. Gradually release pressure on brush to make tail of stroke.

COLOR WASH

A color wash is a light coloration of a project surface. It is similar to Dry Brush, yet creates a softer look that penetrates the project's surface.

To create a color wash, mix one part acrylic paint with two to three parts water. Dip paintbrush in color wash and brush across the area to receive color. Decrease pressure on the brush as you move outward. Repeat as needed to create the desired effect.

CRACKLING

This technique creates a crazed effect on project surface, allowing the basecoat to show through the top coat, which produces an aged effect.

Paint surface with desired basecoat color and allow to dry. Apply an even coat of crackle medium (the thicker the coat of crackle medium, the deeper the cracks). Allow to become tacky, but not dry. Brush on one coat of a second color paint. Cracks will appear following the direction of the topcoat brush strokes.

Other types of crackle medium that are available include one that is applied over two layers of paint and another that comes in colors and is applied over one layer of paint.

DOTS

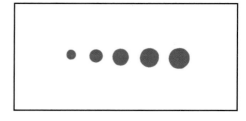

Dip the tip of a round paintbrush, the handle end of a paintbrush, or one end of a toothpick in paint and touch to project. Dip in paint each time for uniform dots.

DOUBLE LOAD

Dip brush into water; blot on paper towel. Dip corner of brush into paint; dip the opposite corner of brush into another shade of paint. Stroke brush on a palette or waxed paper to blend the two shades of paint.

DRY BRUSH

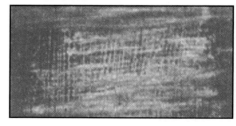

This technique creates a random top coat coloration of a project's surface. It is similar to a Color Wash, yet creates an aged look that sits on top of the project's surface.

Do not dip brush in water. Dip a stipple brush or old paintbrush in paint; wipe most of the paint off onto a dry paper towel. Lightly rub the brush across the area to receive color. Decrease pressure on the brush as you move outward. Repeat as needed to create the desired effect.

FLOATING COLOR

Dip brush in water; blot on a paper towel. Dip corner of brush into paint. Stroke brush back and forth on palette until there is a gradual change from paint to water in each brush stroke. Stroke loaded side of brush along detail line on project, pulling brush toward you and turning project if necessary. For shading, load brush with a darker color of paint. For highlighting, load brush with lighter color of paint.

LINE WORK (PERMANENT PEN)

To prevent smudging lines or ruining pen, let paint dry before beginning line work. Draw over detail lines with permanent pen.

LINE WORK (LINER BRUSH)

Mix paint with water to an ink-like consistency. Dip liner brush into thinned paint. Touch tip of brush to painting surface to outline details.

RUSTING

This technique creates a faux-rusted finish on project's surface.

1. Spray surface of project with a rusty-red color primer.
2. For paints, unevenly mix one part water to one part orange acrylic paint; unevenly mix one part water to one part dark orange acrylic paint.

3. (*Note:* To create a more natural rusted look, use a paper towel or a clean damp sponge piece to dab off paint in some areas after applying paint. Also, drip a few drops of water onto painted surface while paint is still wet, let them run, and then allow to dry.) Dip a dampened sponge into paint; blot on paper towel to remove excess paint. Allowing to dry after each coat, use a light stamping motion to paint project with orange, then dark orange paint mixtures. Apply sealer to project and allow to dry.

SPATTER PAINTING

This technique creates a speckled look on project's surface.

Dip the bristle tips of a dry toothbrush into paint, blot on a paper towel to remove excess, then pull thumb across bristles to spatter paint on project.

SPONGE PAINTING

This technique creates a soft, mottled look on project's surface.

Place project on a covered work surface. Practice sponge-painting technique on scrap paper until desired look is achieved. Paint projects with first color and allow to dry before moving to next color. Use a clean sponge for each additional color.

1. Dampen sponge with water.
2. Dip dampened sponge into paint; blot on paper towel to remove excess paint.
3. Use a light stamping motion to paint project. Allow to dry.
4. If using more than one color of paint, repeat Steps 1 – 3, using a fresh sponge piece for each color.
5. If desired, repeat technique using one color again over areas of other colors, to soften edges or to lighten up a heavy application of one color.

STENCILING

These instructions are written for multicolor stencils. For single-color stencils, make one stencil for the entire design.

1. For first stencil, cut a piece from stencil plastic 1" larger than entire pattern. Center plastic over pattern and use a permanent pen to trace outlines of all areas of first color in stencil cutting key. For placement guidelines, outline remaining colored area using dashed lines. Using a new piece of plastic for each additional color in stencil cutting key, repeat for remaining stencils.
2. Place each plastic piece on cutting mat and use a craft knife to cut out stencil along solid lines, making sure edges are smooth.
3. Hold or tape stencil in place. Using a clean, dry stencil brush or sponge piece, dip brush or sponge in paint. Remove excess paint on a paper towel. Brush or sponge should be almost dry to produce best results. Beginning at edge of cutout area, apply paint in a stamping motion over stencil. If desired, highlight or shade design by stamping a lighter or darker shade of paint in cutout area. Repeat until all areas of first stencil have been painted. Carefully remove stencil and allow paint to dry.
4. Using stencils in order indicated in color key and matching guidelines on stencils to previously stenciled area, repeat Step 3 for remaining stencils.

SEALING

If a project will be handled frequently or used outdoors, we recommend sealing the item with clear sealer. Sealers are available in spray or brush-on form in a variety of finishes. Follow manufacturer's instructions to apply sealer.

Some projects will require two or more coats of sealer. Apply one coat of sealer and allow to dry. Lightly sand with a fine-grit sandpaper then wipe with a tack cloth, before applying next coat.

DÉCOUPAGE

1. Cut desired motifs from fabric or paper.
2. Apply découpage glue to wrong sides of motifs.
3. Arrange motifs on project as desired, overlapping as necessary. Smooth in place and allow to dry.
4. Allowing to dry after each application, apply two to three coats of sealer to project.

SEWING SHAPES

1. Center pattern on wrong side of one fabric piece and use fabric marking pen to draw around pattern. Do not cut out shape.
2. Place fabric pieces right sides together. Leaving an opening for turning, carefully sew pieces together directly on drawn line.
3. Leaving a 1/4" seam allowance, cut out shape. Clip seam allowance at curves and corners. Turn right side out and press. Sew opening closed.

CUTTING A FABRIC CIRCLE

1. Cut a square of fabric the size indicated in project instructions.
2. Matching right sides, fold fabric square in half from top to bottom and again from left to right.
3. Tie one end of string to a pencil or fabric marking pen. Measuring from pencil, insert a thumbtack through string at length indicated in project instructions. Insert thumbtack through folded corner of fabric. Holding tack in place and keeping string taut, mark cutting line (Fig. 1).

Fig. 1

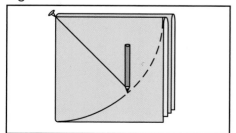

4. Cut along drawn line through all fabric layers.

FUSIBLE APPLIQUÉS

To prevent darker fabrics from showing through, white or light-colored fabrics may need to be lined with fusible interfacing before applying paper-backed fusible web.

To make reverse appliqué pieces, trace pattern onto tracing paper; turn traced paper over and continue to follow all steps using reversed pattern.

1. Use a pencil to trace pattern or draw around reversed pattern onto paper side of web as many times as indicated for a single fabric. Repeat for additional patterns and fabrics.
2. Follow manufacturer's instructions to fuse traced patterns to wrong side of fabrics. Do not remove paper backing.
3. Cut out appliqué pieces along traced lines. Remove paper backing.
4. Arrange appliqués, web side down, on project, overlapping as necessary. Appliqués can be temporarily held in place by touching appliqués with tip of iron. If appliqués are not in desired position, lift and reposition.
5. Fuse appliqués in place.

MACHINE APPLIQUÉ

1. Place paper or stabilizer on wrong side of background fabric under fused appliqué.
2. Beginning on a straight edge of appliqué if possible, position project under presser foot so that most of stitching will be on appliqué. Take a stitch in fabric and bring bobbin thread to top. Hold both threads toward you and sew over them for several stitches to secure; clip threads. Using a medium-width zigzag stitch, stitch over all exposed raw edges of appliqué(s) and along detail lines as indicated in instructions.
3. When stitching is complete, remove stabilizer. Clip threads close to stitching.

EMBROIDERY STITCHES

BACKSTITCH

Referring to Fig. 1, bring needle up at 1; go down at 2. Bring needle up at 3 and pull through. For next stitch, insert needle at 1; bring up at 4 and pull through. Continue working to make a continuous line of stitches.

Fig. 1

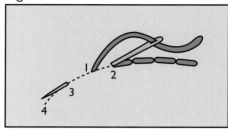

ADDING BEADS

Refer to project design and key for bead placement and sew bead in place using a fine needle that will pass through bead. Bring needle up at 1, run needle through bead and then down at 2. Secure thread on back or move to next bead as shown in Fig. 2.

Fig. 2

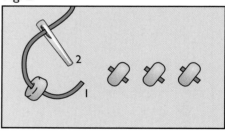

BLANKET STITCH

Bring needle up at 1. Keeping thread below point of needle, go down at 2 and up at 3 (Fig. 3). Continue working as shown in Fig. 4.

Fig. 3

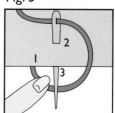

Fig. 4

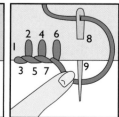

COUCHING

Lay thread to be couched on fabric. With second strand of thread, bring needle up at 1 and go down at 2. Continue making evenly spaced stitches along length of thread (Fig. 5).

Fig. 5

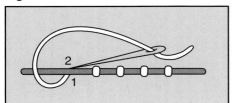

FRENCH KNOT

Bring needle up at 1. Wrap thread once around needle and insert needle at 2, holding thread with non-stitching fingers (Fig. 6). Tighten knot as close to fabric as possible while pulling needle back through fabric.

Fig. 6

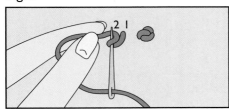

FEATHER STITCH

Bring needle up at 1; keeping thread below point of needle, go down at 2 and come up at 3 (Fig. 7). Go down at 4 and come up at 5 (Fig. 8). Continue working as shown in Fig. 9.

Fig. 7   **Fig. 8**

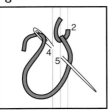

Fig. 9

LAZY DAISY STITCH

Bring needle up at 1; take needle down again at 1 to form a loop and bring up at 2 (Fig. 10a). Keeping loop below point of needle (Fig. 10b), take needle down at 3 to anchor loop.

Fig. 10a   **Fig. 10b**

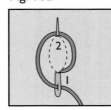

OVERCAST STITCH

Bring needle up at 1; take thread over edge of fabric and bring needle up at 2. Continue stitching along edge of fabric (Fig. 11).

Fig. 11

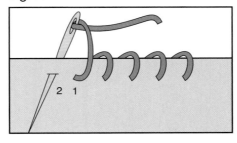

RUNNING STITCH

Referring to Fig. 12, make a series of straight stitches with stitch length equal to the space between stitches.

Fig. 12

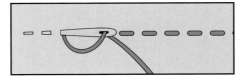

SATIN STITCH

Referring to Fig. 13, come up at odd numbers and go down at even numbers with the stitches touching but not overlapping.

Fig. 13

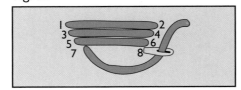

STEM STITCH

Referring to Fig. 14, come up at 1. Keeping thread below stitching line, go down at 2 and come up at 3. Go down at 4 and come up at 5.

Fig. 14

STRAIGHT STITCH

Bring needle up at 1 and take needle down at 2 (Fig. 15). Length of stitches may be varied as desired.

Fig. 15

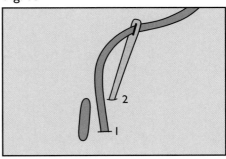

WHIPSTITCH

Bring needle up at 1 and take needle down at 2 (Fig. 16). Continue until opening is closed or trim is attached.

Fig. 16

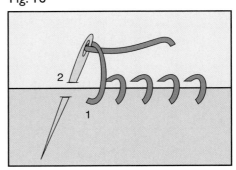

BOWS

SIMPLE BOW

1. For the first streamer, measure and lightly mark 10" from one end of ribbon. For the first loop, begin at streamer mark; measure and lightly mark 8".

2. To form first loop, place first loop mark behind streamer mark; gather ribbon between thumb and forefinger (Fig. 1).

Fig. 1

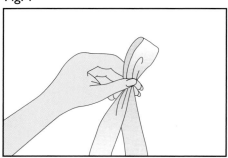

3. Loosely wrap remaining length of ribbon once around thumb (Fig. 2). To form second loop, fold remaining ribbon approximately 4" from end of wrapped area; slide folded end of ribbon through wrapped area.

Fig. 2

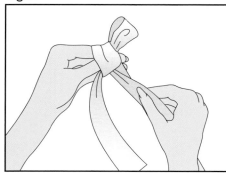

4. Place thumbs inside loops (Fig. 3). Pull the loops to tighten bow. Adjust size of loops by pulling on streamers. Trim streamers.

Fig. 3

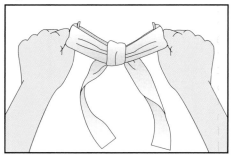

MULTI-LOOP BOW

Note: Loop sizes given in project instructions refer to the length of ribbon used to make one loop of bow. If no size is given, make loops desired size for project.

1. For first streamer, measure desired length of streamer from one end of ribbon; twist ribbon between fingers (Fig. 1).

Fig. 1

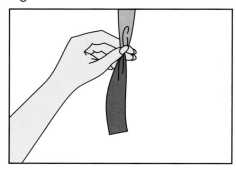

2. Keeping right side of ribbon facing out, fold ribbon to front to form desired-size loop; gather ribbon between fingers (Fig. 2). Fold ribbon to back to form another loop; gather ribbon between fingers (Fig. 3).

Fig. 2

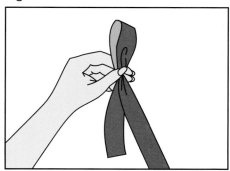

Fig. 3

3. (*Note:* If a center loop is desired, form half the desired number of loops, then loosely wrap ribbon around thumb and gather ribbon between fingers as shown in Fig. 4; form remaining loops.) Continue to form loops, varying size of loops as desired, until bow is desired size.

Fig. 4

4. For remaining streamer, trim ribbon to desired length.

5. To secure bow, hold gathered loops tightly. Fold a length of floral wire around gathers of loops. Hold wire ends behind bow, gathering all loops forward; twist bow to tighten wire. Arrange loops and trim ribbon ends as desired.

MAKING CHOCOLATE CURLS

Making chocolate curls for garnishes is not difficult, but it does take a little practice. The chocolate should be the correct firmness to form the curls, neither too soft nor too hard. Different types of baking chocolates may be used, but the most common ones are semisweet and unsweetened. They are packaged in boxes containing one-ounce squares.

There are several methods for making chocolate curls. To make small, short curls, hold a baking chocolate square in your hand for a few minutes to slightly soften chocolate. Rub chocolate over shredding side (large holes) of a grater to form curls. For medium-size curls, use a vegetable peeler or chocolate curler (available in kitchen specialty shops) to shave the wide side (for wide curls) or thin side (for thin curls) of a chocolate square.

To make long, thin, loosely formed curls, melt 6 chocolate squares and pour into a foil-lined 3 1/4 x 5 1/4-inch loaf pan. Chill until chocolate is set (about 2 hours). Remove from pan and remove foil. Rub chocolate over shredding side (large holes) of a grater to form curls.

To make large curls, melt about 5 chocolate squares and pour into a jellyroll pan or onto a cookie sheet. Spread chocolate over pan. Chill about 10 minutes. Scrape across surface of chocolate with a long metal spatula, knife, teaspoon, or chocolate curler to form curls. The spatula and knife will form long, thin curls and the teaspoon and curler will form shorter curls. Return pan to refrigerator if chocolate becomes too soft. Use a toothpick to pick up curls.

TOASTING NUTS

To toast nuts, spread nuts on an ungreased baking sheet. Stirring occasionally, bake in a 350-degree oven 5 to 8 minutes or until nuts are slightly darker in color.

TESTS FOR CANDY MAKING

To determine the correct temperature of cooked candy, use a candy thermometer and the cold water test. Before each use, check the accuracy of your candy thermometer by attaching it to the side of a small saucepan of water, making sure thermometer does not touch bottom of pan. Bring water to a boil. Thermometer should register 212 degrees in boiling water. If it does not, adjust the temperature range for each candy consistency accordingly.

When using a candy thermometer, insert thermometer into candy mixture, making sure thermometer does not touch bottom of pan. Read temperature at eye level. Cook candy to desired temperature range. Working quickly, drop about 1/2 teaspoon of candy mixture into a cup of ice water. Use a fresh cup of water for each test. Use the following descriptions to determine if candy has reached the correct stage:

Soft-Ball Stage (234 to 240 degrees): Candy can be rolled into a soft ball in ice water but will flatten when removed from water.

Firm-Ball Stage (242 to 248 degrees): Candy can be rolled into a firm ball in ice water but will flatten if pressed when removed from water.

Hard-Ball Stage (250 to 268 degrees): Candy can be rolled into a hard ball in ice water and will remain hard when removed from water.

Soft-Crack Stage (270 to 290 degrees): Candy will form hard threads in ice water but will soften when removed from water.

Hard-Crack Stage (300 to 310 degrees): Candy will form brittle threads in ice water and will remain brittle when removed from water.

SOFTENING BUTTER OR MARGARINE

To soften one stick of butter, remove wrapper and place butter on a microwave-safe plate. Microwave on medium-low power (30%) 20 to 30 seconds.

SOFTENING CREAM CHEESE

To soften cream cheese, remove wrapper and place cream cheese on a microwave-safe plate. Microwave on medium power (50%) 1 to 1 1/2 minutes for an 8-ounce package or 30 to 45 seconds for a 3-ounce package.

ROLLING OUT PIE DOUGH

Use four 24-inch-long pieces of plastic wrap. Overlapping long edges, place 2 pieces of wrap on a slightly damp flat surface; smooth out wrinkles. Place dough in center of wrap. Overlapping long edges, use remaining pieces of wrap to cover dough. Use rolling pin to roll out dough 2 inches larger than diameter of pie plate. Remove top pieces of wrap. Invert dough into pie plate. Remove remaining pieces of wrap.

WHIPPING CREAM

For greatest volume, chill a glass bowl and beaters before beating whipping cream. In warm weather, place chilled bowl over ice while beating whipping cream.

SHREDDING CHEESE

To shred cheese easily, place wrapped cheese in freezer 10 to 20 minutes before shredding.

DISSOLVING DRY YEAST

Use warm water (105 to 115 degrees) when dissolving yeast. Higher temperatures kill yeast and prevent breads from rising properly.

RECIPE INDEX

A

Almond-Bacon-Cheese Crostini, 17
APPETIZERS & SNACKS:
  Almond-Bacon-Cheese Crostini, 17
  Brie in Braided Bread Wreath, 77
  Cranberry Ambrosia-Cream
    Cheese Spread, 81
  Crunchy Cheese Snacks, 85
  Hot Crab Dip, 78
  Mongolian Beef Skewers, 17
  Reindeer Gorp, 110
  Roquefort Firecrackers, 90
  Salmon Tarts, 85
  Smoky Cheese Ball, 85
  Spicy Ginger Cookies, 96
  Tomatoes Rockefeller, 76
Apricot Jewel Cookies, 99

B

Baked Ham with Bourbon Glaze, 75
Bar Essentials, 78
BEEF:
  Creamy Beef Stroganoff, 84
  Mongolian Beef Skewers, 17
  Mushroom-Rosemary
    Beef Tenderloin, 69
BEVERAGES:
  Bar Essentials, 78
  Four-Fruit Wassail, 78
  Holiday Irish Coffee Eggnog, 97
  Hot Cider Nog, 91
  Hot Mulled Fruit Cider, 96
  Perfect Coffee, 81
  Raspberry Cordial, 18
Blonde Brownies with
  Chocolate Chunks, 91
Bread Pudding with
  Whiskey Sauce, 72

BREADS, BISCUITS, & MUFFINS:
  Braided Bread Wreath (Brie in), 77
  Cheese-and-Pepper
    Muffin Mix, 109
  Parsley-Garlic Rolls, 72
  Pecan Cornbread Loaf, 89
  Sour Cream Yeast Rolls, 114
  Spoon Rolls, 18
  Sweet Potato Angel Biscuits, 75
Brie in Braided Bread Wreath, 77
BROWNIES & BARS:
  Blonde Brownies with
    Chocolate Chunks, 91
  Crème de Menthe Bars, 97
  Lemon-Cream Cheese Squares, 86
  Really Raspberry Brownies, 103
Buttermilk Pralines, 105
Butter-Pecan Green Beans, 70

C

CAKES:
  Carrot-Praline Cake, 93
  Holiday Chocolate Log, 81
  Sour Cream-Streusel
    Pound Cake, 86
CANDIES & CONFECTIONS:
  Buttermilk Pralines, 105
  Can't-Fail Divinity, 102
  Chocolate-Praline Truffles, 112
  Pecan Toffee, 102
  Sugar-and-Spice Pecans, 111
Can't-Fail Divinity, 102
Caraway Seed Wafers, 97
Carrot-Praline Cake, 93
CHEESE:
  Almond-Bacon-Cheese Crostini, 17
  Brie in Braided Bread Wreath, 77
  Cheese-and-Pepper
    Muffin Mix, 109
  Cranberry Ambrosia-Cream
    Cheese Spread, 81
  Crunchy Cheese Snacks, 85
  Roquefort Firecrackers, 90
  Smoky Cheese Ball, 85
  Spicy Ginger Cookies, 96
CHEESECAKES:
  Chocolate Espresso Cheesecake, 95
  Coconut-Chocolate-Almond
    Cheesecake, 19
Cheese-and-Pepper Muffin Mix, 109
Chicken-Andouille Gumbo, 89

CHOCOLATE:
  Blonde Brownies with
    Chocolate Chunks, 91
  Chocolate Espresso Cheesecake, 95
  Chocolate Macaroons, 100
  Chocolate-Cherry Swirls, 99
  Chocolate-Dipped
    Coffee Kisses, 104
  Chocolate-Pecan Tassies, 87
  Chocolate-Praline Truffles, 112
  Coconut-Chocolate-Almond
    Cheesecake, 19
  Crème de Menthe Bars, 97
  Holiday Chocolate Log, 81
  Magic Peanut Butter Middles, 100
  Pecan Toffee, 102
  Really Raspberry Brownies, 103
  Reindeer Gorp, 110
Chocolate Espresso Cheesecake, 95
Chocolate Macaroons, 100
Chocolate-Cherry Swirls, 99
Chocolate-Dipped Coffee Kisses, 104
Chocolate-Pecan Tassies, 87
Chocolate-Praline Truffles, 112
Chunky Ham Pot Pie, 83
Cinnamon-Almond-Pecan Pie, 94
Cinnamon-Sugar Angels, 101
Coconut-Chocolate-Almond
  Cheesecake, 19
CONDIMENTS:
  Bourbon Glaze
    (Baked Ham with), 75
  Cranberry Vinaigrette
    (Winter Salad with), 17
  Dijon Dressing
    (Mixed Greens with), 90
  Spicy Southwest Chile Oil, 107
COOKIES:
  Apricot Jewel Cookies, 99
  Caraway Seed Wafers, 97
  Chocolate Macaroons, 100
  Chocolate-Cherry Swirls, 99
  Chocolate-Dipped
    Coffee Kisses, 104
  Cinnamon-Sugar Angels, 101
  Giant Ginger-Oatmeal
    Sorghum Cookies, 104
  Magic Peanut Butter Middles, 100
  Nutty Fingers, 101
  Pound Cake Cookies, 100
  Spicy Ginger Cookies, 96
  Walnut Cookies, 78
Cranberry Ambrosia-Cream
  Cheese Spread, 81
Creamy Beef Stroganoff, 84
Crème de Menthe Bars, 97
Crunchy Cheese Snacks, 85

CREDITS

We want to extend a warm *thank you* to the generous people who allowed us to photograph our projects at their homes.

- *Easy Elegance:* Dan and Jeanne Spencer
- *Lakeside Cabin Christmas:* John and Kit Bakker, Jay and Patsy Hill, and Bill and Lynn Phelps
- *Winter Majesty:* Larry and Carol McAdams and Chris Olsen
- *Naturally Christmas:* Carl and Monte Brunck
- *Flea Market Fancies:* Leighton Weeks

A special word of thanks goes to Et Cetera of Little Rock, Arkansas, for the use of the silver bowl shown on page 41.

Our sincere appreciation goes to photographers Jerry R. Davis of Jerry Davis Photography, Nancy Nolan of Nola Studios, and Mark Mathews of the Peerless Group, all of Little Rock, Arkansas, for their excellent photography. Photography stylists Becky Charton, Sondra Harrison Daniel, Karen Smart Hall, and Charlisa Erwin Parker also deserve a special mention for the high quality of their collaboration with these photographers.

We would like to recognize Viking Husqvarna Sewing Machine Company of Cleveland, Ohio, for providing the sewing machines used to make many of our projects; Therm O Web, Inc., of Wheeling, Illinois, for providing the PeelnStick™ Double Sided Adhesive products used in several of our projects; and Walnut Hollow® Woodcrafts of Dodgeville, Wisconsin, for the clock and clock movement kits used to create the *Découpaged Clock* on page 58.

We are sincerely grateful to Rose Glass Klein, who assisted in making and testing some of the recipes in this book.